向善向上

Towards Kindness, Towards Betterment

玳瑚師父 著
Master Dai Hu

序

　　和弟子及學生，在旺區的日本餐館用晚膳，突然來的手機鈴聲，打斷了吾等的談話。來電者是位本地，數一數二的名錶店女經理，欲找吾擇日新店開張及店面風水堪察。掛電後，吾對弟子及學生「放話」説吾將把網撒得更遠。哪知，今年就正式開始寫作，到現在的「出書」。這彷彿來得甚快，有如迅雷來不及掩耳。

　　這本書命名為《向善向上——我要學好》，是最直接的內心叫喊，不再「一意孤行」地走在錯路上，而是馬上接受「老馬識途」的路人，指引一條回家的正途，浪子回頭金不換。

　　　　大千世界莫流連，向善向上朝聖賢，
　　　　我要學好是真言，伏案寫作非等閒。

　　祝　開卷有益

Foreword

One evening, I was in town, dining and conversing with my disciples and students at a Japanese restaurant, when my phone rang. The caller on the other line was a manager in a top-tier watch company. She requested for my service to select an auspicious date for the opening of a new branch, as well as to do a Feng Shui audit at the new location. After ending the phone call, I told my disciples and students that I was going to cast my net further. Who knows, I started writing regularly this year, and am now about to publish my first book. It happened so fast like the sudden peal of thunder that leaves no time to cover the ears.

This book, titled "Towards Kindness, Towards Betterment-I Want To Be Good", stems straight from the heart. It is the direct inner voice that tells you not to stubbornly continue on the wayward path, to heed the advice of those who has walked the path and point you to the right direction back home. A wayward child that turns over a new leaf is more precious than gold.

Let us not linger any longer in this boundless universe,
And strive towards kindness and betterment,
To the ways of the sages,
"I want to be Good"
Let this be your mantra in this lifetime,

And may this extraordinary book sets you on this path.

May all readers benefit from this book.

個人網址 Website：www.masterdaihu.com
臉書專頁 Facebook page：www.facebook.com/masterdaihu
聯絡號碼 Contact number：+65 90284291

目錄

Contents

序
Foreword   3

從一張名片說起
The Story Beginning from a Namecard   13

一夜夫妻百日恩
A Day Together as Husband and Wife,
Endless Devotion The Rest Of Your Lives   20

人比鬼更可怕
Humans are More Frightening than Ghosts   24

大救渡
The Great Salvation   30

大愛
All-encompassing Love   33

小雨來的正是時候
And The Rain Came at The Right Moment   37

不要忘了你手上的戒指
Don't Forget the Ring On Your Finger   41

不要摧毀自己的命運
Do Not Destroy Your Own Destiny   46

不懷好「孕」
Not Being Able To Conceive   54

勿將生命來糟蹋
Do Not Trample on Your Life   59

天下本無事，庸人自擾之
Much Ado about Nothing   61

心中有佛
Having The Buddha in Your Heart   64

你、妳的「欠影」
Your Shadow of Debt   70

他、她的背影
His and Her Silhouettes   75

向日
Looking Towards the Sun   80

在還沒變之前
Before The Change Unfolds   83

守護靈的正知
The Right Knowledge about Guardian Spirits   87

有拜有保佑
Blessings For The Ones Who Pray   91

占便宜的未來循環
Taking Advantage Of Others & Its Repercussion   95

佛在心頭坐
The Buddha Sits In My Heart 99

你不要的那個小孩還在
The Baby You Did Not Want Is Still Around 105

你知道「我」在等你嗎？
Do You Know "I" am Waiting For You? 110

我是妳、你最好的朋友
I am Your Best Friend 114

我們都曾年輕
We Were Young Once 117

戒定慧
The Three Endeavours of Moral Discipline,
Meditation and Wisdom 120

投奔黑暗的人
The Ones Who Deflect to Darkness 124

供奉神明的真諦
The True Significance of Deity Worship 127

命運之掌控
Take Control of Your Destiny 131

命運加倍苦的人
A Destiny with Twice The Sufferings 135

和陽光約會吧！
Let's Have A Date With The Sunshine! 139

學佛之正
Learn the Righteous Way of the Buddha   142

宗教的真實義
The True Essence of Religion   144

明因果無煩惱
Understand the Law of Karma for a Worry-free Life   148

武動生命
"Martial" Up Your Life!   153

持咒唸佛
Recitation Of The Buddha's Name & Mantra   157

迎接善光的那一天起
From the Day I Received the Light of Virtue   161

是時候修福修德了
Now is the Time to Cultivate your Merits and Morals 165

洗滌業障
Washing Away Negative Karma   168

風調雨順，國泰民安
The Way To a Prosperous & Peaceful Nation with
Favourable Weather   170

修行在個人
Spiritual Cultivation Is Your Own Responsibility   174

修福惜福
Cultivate and Treasure Your Merits   178

借你呆看幾十年
Just For Your Viewing Pleasure 182

真正的有錢人
A Truly Wealthy Person 186

真正的君子
The True Gentleman 189

真愛新春佳節
My Truly Beloved Spring Festival 192

真實的現象
The True Reality 196

財源廣進
Wealth and Prosperity Abound! 200

健康在陰陽
Being Healthy is about Yin & Yang 204

唱首情歌給妳，你聽
Singing A Love Song For You 208

救人等同救己
Saving Others Is Akin To Saving Yourself 212

清明時節談孝親
Filial Piety on Qingming Festival 215

牽引你向道
Guiding You to the Way 220

被殺前的恐懼，您懂嗎？
Do You Know the Fear Before Being Killed? 222

富與貧的學問
The Knowledge Behind Wealth & Poverty 226

最苦的人
The Person With The Most Sufferings 230

最靠近我們的神靈
The Deity Nearest to Us 232

登山觀浮雲
Watching the Clouds From the Mountains 235

給國家領袖的祝福
My Wishes for Our Country's Leader 241

愚孝愚愛
The Ignorance of Fillial Piety and Love 245

感恩的真諦
The True Essence Of Gratitude 249

電梯受困記
Being Trapped in The Elevator 251

蒼天是否變了心
Did the Heavens have a change of heart? 255

銜接聖誕節的意義
Christmas Day-Connecting the Dots 259

慶生的意義
The Significance Of a Birthday Celebration 262

緣
Affinity 265

緣近緣遠，緣深緣淺
Affinity Near and Afar, Affinity Deep and Shallow 268

學佛
Learning Buddhism 272

學佛的出發心
Motivation for Learning the Dharma 277

樹兒的低語
The Gentle Whispers Of The Trees 281

從一張名片說起
The Story Beginning from a Namecard

　　這一輩子，吾沒想過要出名。對佛法和玄學的熱忱，讓我廢寢忘食地去鑽研。但吾所鑽研的，被很多人慣例地歸爲迷信。本想跑到深山隱居，就這樣過一輩子。如果不是一位老師姐說：「玳瑚啊！你不要再躲了。眾生需要你！」又想到皈依時，根本上師說要奉法持戒，吾早就無知地成爲一位自了漢。

　　於是吾走出來了。

　　第一張名片，是一位弟子在 2002 年時的供養。她說有名片，比較容易介紹吾給別人。吾本不要，但她的一句話觸動了吾的心：「師父，你幫我這麼多，可以讓我爲你做一點事嗎？」

　　「好啦！印幾張就好。」

　　「師父，沒有幾張的。一次就得印三盒！」

　　2007 年，有感自己的名片需要改革了。好些年輕客人的華文不好，不太讀得懂吾的名片。偶爾，也會有非華人的客人。於是，一位年輕女客人義務爲吾操刀，依據吾的要求，加上中英文字體，做出新的設計。

　　弟子問：「師父，爲什麼您名片的蓮花有莖？佛教裡繪畫的蓮花，不都沒有莖嗎？」

　　吾答：「這蓮花有莖代表有紮實的底，如師父有很深厚

13

功夫一樣，一步一腳印應證出來的，絕不是個馬馬虎虎的師父。二，師父這蓮花的莖是要植入眾生的心裡，希望師父的教誨能讓他們得到清涼，帶領他們離苦得樂。」

第一次將新的名片給一位舊客人時，他說：「喔！師父開始商業化了。」

吾笑笑不語。人和人之間，往往就是因為先入為主而產生了誤會。

2008 年，弟子問：「師父，不如我幫您設個臉書專頁？現在很多人必讀的書就是臉書！很多師父也在網上傳達佛理和玄學。可以將您的教義傳的更遠更廣，利益更多人！」

吾當時一口拒絕。吾自認文筆平平、相貌平平，在網絡上不會有作為。憶起當年舊客人的話，更有所顧慮。怎知弟子不到黃河心不死，每隔一段日子就嘗試說服吾，什麼大道理都講盡。天啊！原來有那麼長氣的弟子！吾的耳根……

2012 年四月，臉書專頁成立了。2013 年九月二十八日，發了第一篇文章〈電梯受困記〉。

今天這篇是第六十六篇文章了。一年來，結交了不少朋友，有舊雨也有新知，有素昧平生的，也有已失去聯絡的卻奇妙地在網上搜尋到吾的臉書專頁。有新馬的朋友，也有港臺、菲律賓和澳洲的朋友。（網絡世界不可思議。）有的讀華文，有的只讀英文，有的雙語兼讀。每位按「讚」的，每有新的粉絲，弟子都會給吾看。

許多時候，吾會對著那手機螢幕輕聲地說「謝謝你」。

謝謝妳、你的喜歡。謝謝妳、你的轉發。謝謝妳、你的推薦。

弟子問：「師父，你現在寫文章是爲了什麼而寫？」

「履行吾的願，弘揚佛法和玄學。」

「那有多少個『讚』會影響你嗎？」

「沒有去想，無爲而爲。寫了就是了。」

一人也好，多人也罷，只要能帶一份清涼給妳、你，吾就會繼續地揮筆洒墨！

—— 英譯 ——

In this lifetime, fame has not been something which I pursue. The passion I have for Buddhism and Chinese Metaphysics see me delving deep into research, often foregoing my meals and sleep for it. However, there are a lot of people who habitually dismissed my passion as superstition. I thought of leading a reclusive life for the rest of my life. Had it not for a fellow Dharma sister who told me, "Dai Hu! Please don't hide anymore. The sentient beings need you!", as well as my Root Guru's words to uphold the precepts and the Dharma, I would have ignorantly become a recluse.

Because of their words, I decided to step out.

My first proper name card was a gift from a disciple in the

year 2002. She said it would be easier to recommend me to others if I had a name card. I refused initially, but something she said touched me. "Master, You have helped me tremendously. Will you please let me do something for you?"

"Alright! Just print a few pieces will do"

"Master, I cannot print a few pieces. It has to be three boxes!", she said.

In 2007, I saw the need to redesign my name card. A lot of my younger clientele do not have a competent grasp of Mandarin and cannot understand the information on my name card. Occasionally, I do have non-Chinese clients too. Thus, a young lady client of mine offered her assistance and designed my new name card, according to my requirements, and with English and Chinese information.

A disciple asked, "Master, why does the lotus drawing in your name card have a stem? Is it not that the lotus, usually depicted in Buddhism illustrations, has no stem?"

I answered, "The stem of the lotus signifies a solid grounding, just as I diligently honed my skills over the years. I am definitely not a Master that is shoddy with his work. Secondly, the stem of the lotus is to penetrate the

heart of all sentient beings. I hope that my teachings will provide a breeze of purity and clarity to them, and guide them out of sufferings and to eternal bliss."

The very first time I gave my new name card to an old client, he said, "Oh, Master is getting more commercialized!"

I just smiled and kept mum. Often between people, we fall into the trap of preconceptions that eventually create misunderstandings.

In 2008, my disciple proposed, "Master, why not I help you create a Facebook page? Nowadays, the book that everyone read is Facebook! There are many Masters propagating the Dharma and Chinese metaphysics online. You can use the Internet to spread your teachings further and wider to benefit more people!"

I turned her proposal down flat. At that time, I deemed my own writing skills as average at best and coupled with my ordinary looks, I did not think I would achieve anything online. The words of my old client added to my misgivings. Surprisingly, this disciple of mine refused to take no for an answer, and would preach to me about having an online presence every other day, with all the reasons that she could think of. My goodness! How did I end up having such a long-winded disciple? My poor ears…

In April 2012, my Facebook Page was set up. On 28th September 2013, my first article, titled Trapped in the Lift, was posted.

This Facebook post marks the 66th article, since inception, which I have shared with my readers. Over the past year, I have made many friends on Facebook, both old and new. There are some whom I have never met, and there are others who found my Facebook page online after losing touch for a long time. There are Facebook friends from Singapore, Malaysia, as well as from Hong Kong, Taiwan, Philippines and Australia. (The Internet is incredible.) Some read the articles in Mandarin, some only consume the English ones and there are those who pore over both versions.

Every time there is a new "Like" or a new fan to my page, my disciple would show me the notifications with her mobile phone.

Many a time, I will gently say "Thank you" whilst looking at the screen. Thank you all for the likes. Thank you all for the shares. Thank you all for the recommendations.

My disciple asked, "Master, nowadays, what keeps you writing?"

My answer to her, "I am carrying out my promise, to propagate the Dharma and Chinese metaphysics."

"Does the number of 'likes' affect you?"

"It does not cross my mind. I do what I should do, do it well and let things run its own course."

Be it only a single reader, or many, as long as my writings can give you inner peace and relief from your troubles, I will continue to wield my pen!

一夜夫妻百日恩

A Day Together as Husband and Wife, Endless Devotion The Rest Of Your Lives

　　吾，玞瑚師父，當然見過恩愛的夫妻，也當然見過歡喜冤家的夫妻，以及……。無論恩不恩愛，合與不合，依然是「緣」。難道妳、你不知道，夫妻本是五百年前的冤家嗎？就因如此，「天下有情人終成眷屬」，但天下少有百年佳偶。既然如此，冤家宜解不宜結才對啊！不該干戈四起，殃及他人才是啊！

　　批過眾多的八字中，是有為數不少的八字隱藏婚姻危機，及伴侶危機。怎麼有這麼多的危機呢？要知道有因必有果，有果必有因。這些危機是妳、你「之前」，所造下的，「之後」機緣成熟也自然就會有那般這般的「機遇」呀！真正的智者是理清，這「之前」與「之後」的道理再從現實生活中給於修繕，「家庭和諧」才能夠有朝一日實現。

　　玞瑚師父實實在在告訴大家，就因為多世的「緣分」，其實是業緣才對，才有這麼的「是是非非」，彼此的敵對、欺騙及傷害，就讓你們去修正，然後全部都不會再降生在這「吵吵鬧鬧」的世界裡，反而生在清淨、快樂、自在、一切俱足的極樂世界裡，絕對沒有悲傷、敵對、爭執、痛苦與煩惱，只有笑呵呵、富足及永恆的快樂。

夫妻一定要真心，好好的對待彼此，要記得一夜夫妻百日恩，心要常存感激及感恩，所謂的「狐狸精」，又或者「小三」又如何「有機可乘」呢？倘若妳、你還是「無法渡」（福建話），玳瑚師父歡迎妳、你將妳、你的伴侶送來玳瑚師父「培訓班」，接受玳瑚師父充滿愛心、耐心、智慧之教化，使妳、你個人與家庭生機連年。

—— 英譯 ——

I, Master Dai Hu, have seen many loving and devoted married couples, as well as a fair share of couples with mixed fortunes in their marriages. Regardless of their level of devotion, love or compatibility with each other, it all boils down to the affinity between them. Are you not aware that a married couple was once enemies with each other five hundred years ago? Thus there is this phrase "May all lovers in this world be united in wedlock". However, it is rare to find a harmonious couple that can last a hundred years. Therefore, it is wise to resolve any enmity and not create new ones. There is no need to break out into a war and hurt others!

After analyzing countless birth charts, there are indeed

many cases where the danger signs to a marriage as well as to your partner are hidden. Why would there be so many danger signs? You must know that for every effect, there is always a cause, and vice versa. These danger signs were the effects of the negative causes that you have created in the past. A person with true wisdom will have clarity of this Law of Cause and Effect, and work hard in his or her present life to improve the situation and achieve harmony in the family soonest.

Master Dai Hu tells everyone truthfully that these affinities, negative ones I should say, accumulated over numerous lifetimes culminate in the disharmony in your relationships this lifetime. The instances of slandering, enmity, deceit and hurt gives you the opportunity to resolve them and not have them happen again and again. Once resolved, none of you will be entangled in this endless noise of samsara (cycle of births and deaths), but instead, you will be reborn in the Pure Land, where all is pure, happiness, bliss and abundance. There will be no sorrow, enmity, discord, pain and sufferings. Only laughter, prosperity and eternal happiness.

A husband and wife must be true towards each other and treat each other well. They must remember that a day together as husband and wife means endless devotion to each other for the rest of their lives. Always be thankful and grateful for each other. In this way, how will the "vixen" or third party have any chance to come between both of you? If you are still at your wit's end, Master Dai Hu welcomes you to send your partner to my training class to learn my teachings of love, patience and wisdom, and bring back the bliss and happiness to your personal and family life.

人比鬼更可怕

Humans are More Frightening than Ghosts

　　去年吾有寫過一篇有關農曆七月「鬼節」的文章。雖然「鬼節」剛過，我依然在此為你們介紹人與鬼「不為人知」的一面。

　　在近半百的人生歲月裡，吾所接觸過的人，其數之多實不在話下。而吾的工作也必須接見很多很多人。因此，對於人的「人性」，有吾最真實的認知。坦白說，吾是較怕人多過於鬼。蓋人的性格，並不鮮明。幫了她、他之後，不求她、他的回報，但求她、他不會反回頭咬吾就好。相信吾這樣的說法，在在都有共鳴。

　　這裡就披露幾則發生在吾及吾眾多客人身上的真實事情，讓妳、你們參考，人的「人性」，何為不鮮明。有位弟子的父親，為了要讓其子國外攻讀碩士學位，毅然將賣屋的錢，圓其兒子的「夢」。這兒子的「夢」是圓了，可是至今仍然沒有感恩的心、盡孝父母、回饋社會，反而還跟父親慪氣、冷戰，甚至自私自利地不管父母弟妹的未來生死問題。養兒防老，看來是養兒煩惱啊！哀哉其父。記得最初見這位弟子時，著實有點驚嚇。因其臉相有如「惡人谷」出來的。但吾依然收他為徒，希望他能夠認真學佛，清除累世的業障及現世心中的垃圾。吾的天真卻忘了「相由心生」這句話。後來他果然常犯戒，更嚴重的是，他既然不把戒律放在眼裡，一錯再錯，如今罪如山、過如海，再不速速懺悔重新受

戒，恐怕悔時已晚。

　　另有一學生，也是碩士生。雖有碩士學位，可是卻失業，也找不到就業機會。吾知道後，馬上二話不說的，親自出馬運用玄學的力量，為他謀得現今這份高職，並且授予他真實的佛法與基本玄學，好讓他從中體悟人生實相、生命實相以及福份次第的種種。至今他每次來上課，都會有新的怨言及新的欲望。（感恩的人，不會有怨言。）吾想，他是男的沒錯。可是怎麼「怨」力如此大，宛如怨婦再來，真是阿彌陀佛啊！做男不容易，難道你想做女不成？受人恩惠，不圖回報，還成天打妄語、怨這怨那的，再這樣下去，人身不保，三途惡道等著你。速醒，速醒。

　　有位客戶來電欲批八字。吾問為何？她答欲找新工作，因與公司經理不和。她好意幫經理處理鐘長的問題，哪知反遭經理「盯死」。她覺得這樣做下去沒意思。這是「狗咬呂洞賓，不識好人心」。另有位美麗的空姐，因丈夫不忠，找吾堪輿其陽宅，想生個寶寶來「圓滿」婚姻。不久後，果然得了個女娃。吾認為不忠就是不專一，因從專一努力，婚姻才能真正圓滿。

　　鬼的性格較鮮明，在於鬼大多數是直腸子。妳、你祗要幫過她、他一次，她、他一定等待機會來報答妳、你。不像人的心理如此的歪曲。幫了她、他，不求她、他回報，但求她、他不會轉回頭，反咬妳、你就好。因此，吾認為人比鬼更可怕。妳、你認為呢？哈！哈！哈！

I wrote an article about the Hungry Ghosts' Festival around the same time last year. Even though the festival has passed, I am still going to introduce the less known sides of a human and a spirit.

As I approached the half-century mark in my life, as part of my job scope, I have interacted with countless number of people. Thus I possess a thorough appreciation of the human nature. Frankly speaking, I am more afraid of a human than a ghost. The human nature is not pure. When I helped a person, I do not expect him to return any favour. Instead I will be glad if this person does not turn around and harm me. I believe many of you would resonate with my sentiments.

Here, I shall divulge some stories which happened to people around me, to allow you a closer examination of the human nature which is primarily clouded. One of my disciples got his dreams of overseas studies fulfilled when his father sold their home and raised enough funds. This student had his wish but remains an utter ingrate, one who is unfilial to his parents and does not bother with contribution to the society whatsoever. Instead, he scoffs at his father, is constantly at odds with him and sports a selfish attitude towards the spiritual mortality issues of his parents and siblings. Raise a

son to guard against old age? Seemed to me like "raise a son to give you more troubles at old age!" I pity the father. I remember the first day I met this student and was slightly shocked. His face resembled that of a villain from the fictional notorious Bandits Valley. But I still took him in as my disciple, hoping that he will change by learning the Dharma and eradicating the bad karma and all the filthy thrash from his heart. Alas, I was naive to ignore that a person's appearance stems from his very heart. In the end, he flouted all the precepts, belittled them even and continued his errant ways. Now, his bad karma has accumulated as high as the highest mountains, and as deep as the deepest seas. If he does not repent now, I am afraid it will be too late.

Another student was jobless for some time, despite having a Masters. I got to know of it and immediately applied the principles of Chinese Metaphysics on him and eventually landed him his current high post job. In addition, I endowed upon him actual knowledge of Buddhism and the basics of Chinese Metaphysics, in hope that he will see the truth of life and understand the different levels of merits. Till today, whenever he comes for my lessons, I would hear new complaints, grudges or new desires. (A grateful person is not prone to complaining.) I thought to myself, he is a man alright, but he is so full of complaints, just like a vengeful woman! Amituofo! It is not easy to be born a man. Does he really want to be a woman instead? He receives kindness from others with no reciprocation, but instead frequently lies and complains. If this carries on, he will lose his human form in his next life. The three lower realms awaits. Please wake up urgently!

A client called me, requesting for an analysis of her birth chart to be done. I asked her for the reason. She replied that she needed help to look for a new job, due to her current job dissatisfaction. She helped her manager with good intention but ended up being misunderstood and picked on. She felt it was not worth staying on. As the Chinese saying goes, "The dog that bit Master Lu Dong Bin does not realise his kind heartedness". Another client, a beautiful flight attendant, got me to audit the Feng Shui of her house in a bid to save her crumpling marriage, due to her husband's infidelity. She wished for a baby to complete the family. With my help, she had a baby girl not long affter. I feel that being unfaithful is akin to losing one's focus. To diligently keep oneself focused is the key to a blissful marriage.

Ghosts, on the other hand, are much clearer and more direct in their intentions. As long as you have helped a spirit before, the spirit would be sure to repay your kindness, unlike humans with their warped psyche. Do not expect a fellow human to repay your kindness all the time. You would be lucky if he or she does not return your favour with

malice! Thus I feel that a human is far more sinister than a spirit. Don't you think so? Ha ha ha!

大救渡
The Great Salvation

　　有弟子問：「師父，請問您爲何寫文章？」吾回答：「行願。」很早以前，吾就在佛菩薩前發願；弟子玳瑚願將所學的佛法及玄學同步利益諸有情。所以吾才回答行願，行向佛菩薩所發的願。其實啊！這也是佛弟子，原本本該做的事。這樣也才算是眞眞正正的佛教徒，上求佛果，下化眾生。行願更是學習及鍛鍊自己，做個有信用的人。

　　未學佛前，所有眾生皆有貪、嗔、癡、妒、慢、疑（六毒），而這六毒也就是六道輪迴的因。學佛後的眾生，就得精進不懈地盡除，這阻礙我們成佛，離苦得樂的因。就算妳、你始終都不知成佛是怎麼一回事，妳、你祇想「快樂」，妳、你也必需先將這六毒滅除，快樂才能常伴妳、你左右啊！

　　試想想，妳、你起初說要賺一百萬，一百萬得到了，妳、你又說再賺多一百萬就退休，哪知前一百萬妳、你已耗掉巨大的時間與精力，後來的一百萬，妳、你所耗掉的，一定不只巨大的時間與精力，當中還必賠上妳、你的健康、家庭、伴侶、子女以及修行機緣。更何況，做生意必涉及貪、嗔、癡、妒、慢、疑，殺、盜、淫、妄、酒，財、色、名、食、睡，這些再再都是墮落六道輪迴受苦的因啊！

　　玳瑚師父已得此智慧，也老早展開「大救渡」的工作，

若妳、你願意的話，歡迎妳、你跟我來。

My disciple asked, "Master, what is your purpose in writing the articles?"

My reply was "To fulfil my vows."

A long time ago, I made a vow to the Buddhas and Bodhisattva that I would bring benefits to all sentient beings, with my knowledge of Buddhadharma and Chinese Metaphysics. Thus, my reply to my disciple. In all truthfulness, this is what all Buddhists ought to be doing, to live up to the name of being a Buddhist, one who seeks the fruits of enlightenment and delivers salvation to all sentient beings. The process of fulfilling your vows enriches your mind and trains your will to be a trustworthy person.

Before learning the Dharma, all of us possess the six poisons, namely greed, wrath, ignorance, jealously, arrogance and suspicion. These six poisons are the very causes of our never-ending journey in the six realms of existence. As we learn the Dharma, we should display utmost diligence to eradicate these obstacles to our enlightenment and liberation from sufferings. Even though you may have no idea of what it means to be a Buddha and all you want is happiness, you will still need to eradicate these six poisons before true happiness can be experienced.

Think about it, you had wanted to make your first million dollars. What happened after you had achieved it? You said you need another million before you will retire. But you had already sacrificed an enormous amount of time and energy for your first million and in the pursuit for more, you are bound to lose your health, family, spouse, kids and the opportunity for spiritual cultivation. Furthermore, in the business world, it is inevitable that you will be tainted by greed, wrath, ignorance, jealously, arrogance, suspicion and unwholesome acts and thoughts of killing, stealing, lust, false speech and alcohol consumption. Not to mention the temptations of wealth, lust, fame, good food and sloth. These are the causes of falling into the six realms of reincarnation and having to undergo suffering!

Master Dai Hu has gained the wisdom of this truth and had long began the work of the great salvation. If you are willing, you are welcome to join me.

大愛
All-encompassing Love

　　青春年少時，非常期盼與渴望，能擁有一份純潔、永恆的愛。而吾所謂的愛，不單單指兩性之間的愛，而是包括友情及親情。可是這些憧憬，仍然只是憧憬。內心深處，是有些淒淒然與無奈，為何總是遇不到真愛。

　　真愛是遇不到，但慶倖吾生在一個有信仰的家庭，年少時也有了宗教及玄學的因緣。這兩大的因緣，淺移默化地啟發吾的智慧，並滋潤吾的心靈，讓吾不至於變成不理智，且有報復及怨恨心的人。吾著實感恩宗教與玄學。

　　在漫長的學習與實修的歲月裡，吾的領悟是這樣的：一般人以為有了伴侶，好好愛他，就是愛了。他們也認為這種愛已是很偉大了。聽起來是沒有錯，但大家仔細地想一想，一位要將她的愛平均分給十個孩子的母親，一位無微不至地照顧整間醫院的醫生，更甚的是，一位天天無時無刻為一切眾生祈禱的宗教領袖，他們所付出的愛，相對於兩性之間的愛，試問那一種愛比較偉大？相信無須吾說，仁人君子，已知曉答案。

　　當然，我們今天不是在比較誰的愛較大，而是要告知大家大愛的重要性。你們可知道為何有宗教之間的不和諧，為何有恐怖分子，為何有戰爭，等等。這一切都是因為沒有大愛啊！如果說，全世界的人類是上帝所造，那人類的自相殘

殺，難道是上帝所要看到的？千萬不可罵天，也千萬不可憑空亂想。祂如果沒有大愛，祂是不能成為上帝的。

今日今時，玳瑚師父能「安枕無憂」，乃是因為吾已體悟大愛，並且願吾在有生之年，能傳達大愛精神，使這世間多些祥和之氣。沒有大愛的地方肯定是比較動亂不安的。安定的生活，是每一個人都想過的。既然如此，何不大家共同打造，真正「欣欣向榮」的未來？來吧！大家一起來吧！來釋放及施展在妳、你心中深處的大愛。

──── 英譯 ────

In my youth, I craved and hoped for a pure and everlasting love. My perception of love was not limited to the romantic pursuits between two lovers. It encompassed friendships and kinships as well. Alas, my longings remained unfulfilled. Deep inside me were just feelings of despair and helplessness that true love somehow eluded me.

I did not meet my true love but fortune favoured me to be born in a religious family and I got to know Chinese Metaphysics and religion when I was young. These two studies imperceptibly inspired me and nurtured my soul. My wisdom grew and it prevented me from turning into an irrational and vengeful person. I am truly grateful to Buddhism and Chinese Metaphysics.

As I walked the long long road of learning and actualising my practice, I form this understanding: it is a common notion that if a person finds his or her other half, and loves him or her proper, that is it. That is their definition of love. It does not sound wrong, but let's just think a little deeper. A mother who shares her love among her ten children. A doctor who takes very good care of his patients in a hospital. And a religious leader who relentlessly prays everyday for the well-being of all sentient beings. Which kind of love is more noble, as compared to the former between two persons? I rest my case, and I know the wise one in you already have the answer.

Of course, we are not comparing whose love is more significant, but more importantly to let everyone knows the importance of great love. Do you know the reason for disharmony between the different religions? Why are there terrorists and wars etc? All these boil down to the lack of agape love! If God creates all beings, He would not like to see us killing one another. Do not blame God nor let your imagination run wild. If He does not have agape love, He would not be God.

At present, Master Dai Hu is able to sleep peacefully because I have truly understood the essence of an all-encompassing love. I sincerely hope that in my future years, I would be able to promote this concept of love and bring more peace and harmony to this world. A place without love is surely not a harmonious place. I am sure everyone wants to lead a peaceful life. Since that is the case, why not join our hands to build a world of harmony and prosperity? Come on! Let us all set free and express the great love that is hidden deep inside everyone of us.

小雨來的正是時候
And The Rain Came at The Right Moment

　　吾對於雨，並沒有特別的喜歡，或特別的討厭。對於雨的認知，吾想也是一知半解吧！那為何寫有關雨的文章呢？這篇雨的文章，是和大家分享吾學佛參禪後，對於雨的感慨，也借這篇文章，傳達雨悄然的貢獻。

　　某夜，見了客人之後，與徒弟和學生到鬧區的某間餐室享用夜宵。我們享用各自的食物，我們也談了一些話題。在不知不覺中，有一絲絲的涼意，從四面八方漂來，周圍的氣氛，添加了多一份的寧靜。心想在這樣的場合，怎有這可能。於是，就將頭兒往左邊探。啊……原來是下雨了。頓時心中有了靈感，頓時對雨有了感懷。而這篇文章的因緣在此。

　　若您不介意，吾非常願意，將吾對於雨的感懷通過文字呈獻給您。那天所下的小雨，真的是小雨來得正是時候啊！因為它不只是增添外觀上的美感，它也不只是將酷熱的氣溫降低而已，它更能沖淡吾對眾生過多的「憂傷」。它也讓吾心中的「熱惱」得到慰藉。雨，它原來早已成為吾的「默友」。我們不常「通訊」，但它卻很懂吾的心。因為它來的時候，彷彿都是吾想見它的時候，也是吾較有空向它微笑，打招呼的時候。它也知曉吾較欣賞有禮貌的人。因此，它也甚少「突然出現」在吾的眼前。

眞慚愧，吾活到這把年歲，才會眞正體悟雨的善、雨的美、雨的細心、雨的懂事、雨的內涵，等等。雨，玳瑚懇請你的原諒，原諒這總是比人慢的孩子，在你細心的灌漑下，會比昨日更積極、更堅強及更發心，學習你普被天下生靈，偉大無私之精神。雨，虔心感謝你耐心的「點醒」吾這愚笨的孩子。讓吾這「問題」孩子，繼續爲「明心見性」而奮鬥。

　　希望所有觀讀這篇文章的你，妳，一樣有小雨來的正是時候，清涼之覺受。

英譯

I used to have a neutral feeling towards rain. Neither do I have a lot of appreciation for it. Why, then, is this article about rain? Well, my main purpose is to share with everybody my changed perspective on rain after I started my spiritual cultivation. Through this article, I hope to highlight the quiet contribution of the rain.

One night after I am done with my consultations, my students and I went for supper at the town area. We were having our own meals, engaging in light conversations, when I felt a wisp of cool breeze swaying in from all directions. A surreal sense of tranquility engulfed the surroundings which, at that moment, had me baffled. I tilted

my head slightly to my left and realised that it was the rain. Momentarily, an inspiration arose, a feeling towards the rain was formed, thus this article.

If you do not mind, I would be most willing to share with you my sentiments towards the rain, through this article. The light drizzle that night came at the right moment. Not only did it add an aesthetic beauty to the surrounding, it drove away the heat as well. It diluted my "sorrow" towards sentient beings and calmed the "woes" burning in my heart. Rain has long since become my silent friend. We do not "communicate" often, but it knows me well because it always appears when I wish to see it most and when I have the time to offer it my subtle smile and nod of acknowledgement. It knows that I appreciate good manners, thus it rarely appears in front of me abruptly.

Ashamedly, only at this age do I have a full contemplative understanding of the rain: its kindness, its beauty, its conscientiousness, its maturity, its depth etc. Oh rain, I ask for your forgiveness. Please forgive the dim child in me. With your conscientious shower of nurturing, I will be more motivated, strong-willed and committed in learning your selfless and noble spirit towards all beings. I thank you sincerely for patiently arousing this dim child from his ignorance. This "problem child" will continue his relentless pursuit of Enlightenment.

For all who read this article, I hope you will feel the same cool breeze through your burdened heart, when the rain arrives.

不要忘了你手上的戒指
Don't Forget the Ring On Your Finger

　　有男客人向我埋怨太太如何不賢淑，家裡老是打理不好。也有女客人投訴先生錢賺不多又不體恤她的辛勞。有客人雇用我的服務，因為想知道破裂的婚姻是否能挽回。也有男客人在深夜播電向我哭訴太太無法原諒他的婚外情而遭逐出家門。更有夫妻各自「精彩」後，來問我如何是好。

　　我的副業，仿佛就是家庭輔導官。

　　結婚前，要想清楚，最好能夠請個專業可靠的師父來分析彼此的八字是否匹配。結婚了，就不要貪戀外頭的「風景」。不要以為有很多仰慕者就很有面子，一不謹慎，叫你賠了夫人又折兵。有客人問我為什麼某某某那麼風流，卻還那麼有錢。試問凡夫怎麼看得懂因果呢？他家裡有問題，難道會告訴你嗎？孽障之事不是不報，只是時辰未到。

　　人非聖賢，確實難免會犯錯。最重要是不要重倒覆轍。當對方犯錯時，你要去想想她、他過去怎樣對你好，試著去包容原諒。夫妻之間如果沒有縫，第三者怎麼進的來？有時，需要檢討的是自己的過失。

　　人為什麼會做錯事？因為心裡沒有主。我常鼓勵客人給自己生命一個機會。如果夫妻之間能有共同的信仰，那更好。宗教讓我們深刻地明瞭對與錯、是與非，並給予我們智慧和定力去面對人間的種種誘惑。

有些夫妻本來是恩恩愛愛的，但一搬進新家後，問題就來了，總是為了一些小事便吵起來，孩子越來越難教，之間的距離越來越大，導致一發不可收拾。這是家居風水嚴重出了問題。無奈現代夫妻寧可花萬元在新穎的屋內設計和名牌包飾，也不願投資千元百元在優秀的風水以保障他們的未來。有客人說伴侶不信玄學，但沒有研究就說不信，不也是迷著於不信嗎？

我常告訴客人，當你們吵架時，要想到你們手上的戒指。當初為什麼要戴？你曾經給過對方的一個承諾，為什麼現在會這樣？結婚是自己選的，能夠在一起，就該好好地相處，不要成天吵吵鬧鬧的，利用在一起的緣分去做一些有意義的事情，不是更好嗎？當下就惜緣惜福吧！

祝願所有的夫妻家庭圓滿、共同推廣菩提事業、利己利他、快樂吉祥！

—— 英譯 ————————————————

I get some male clients complaining about their better half. They grumble that their wives are not virtuous enough, with their homes poorly kept. My female clients also have their fair shares of grouses on their partners too. Be it the low income of the husband, or the lack of appreciation on the effort put into the marriage and home by the wife. There are clients who engaged my services to see if their broken marriages can be salvaged; I received calls from male

clients in the middle of the night, weeping that they got booted out of the house because of their infidelity. There were even cases of both partners committing infidelities, and asked me how to keep their marriage from there on.

I seem to have unknowingly became a family counsellor on the sideline.

I urge everyone to have a serious think-through before committing yourself to marriage. It is in the best interest of both parties to engage a professional geomancer to determine the degree of compatibility based on the birth charts of the couple. Once married, steer clear from external temptations. Having lots of admirers may make you feel good but a single missed step will result in an ugly ending for you. A common question I get from clients is regarding the law of karma. They are puzzled as to why some people are committing acts of sexual misconduct yet still enjoying great wealth. My answer will be: The universal law of karma is always fair, we just need patience for the time and conditions to ripen.

Human is by no means a saint, thus to err is definitely human. Importantly, we should not repeat our mistakes. When we face our loved ones whose misdeed has hurt us, think of the good that they have done for us. Empathize with their own weaknesses and seek to forgive them. In self-retrospect, if there were no fault lines or cracks in a marriage, a third party would not appear.

Why do human beings make mistakes? Because of the lack of a guiding light. If a couple share the same faith, it is most beneficial as they will share a deep and common understanding on the definition of right and wrong, providing the wisdom and conviction to face the many temptations of the world.

A lot of couples started out very lovingly, but things take a turn for the worse when they move into a new house. Little things become unbearable, sparking quarrels. The kids became "monsters" and everyone in the family drift apart. This is obviously a huge issue with the new house and its Feng Shui. It is such a pity to see that couples who will not think twice about splurging tens of thousands on the renovation & branded bags & watches, but flinch at the thought of investing a thousand or hundreds on good Feng Shui to secure their family future. Some clients say their partners give the excuse of not being superstitious and do not wish to believe in Feng Shui. In my humble opinion, writing off the art & science of Feng Shui without doing proper study into this field strikes me as the truly superstitious ones!

I frequently advise my clients, that when they get into

quarrels with their partner, take a step back and think of the ring on your finger. Remember you chose your own marriage. Go back to the time when it all began, and remember the purity of the promise you made. It is affinity that brings two persons together and you should make good use of the definite period of time together. Instead of shouting and fighting all day long, make a change. Isn't it better to do something meaningful together and make the world a better place? Let's start by cherishing being together!

It is my ardent wish for all couples to have a blessed and happy marriage and together embark on a meaningful journey of contributing to the common good of humanity!

不要摧毀自己的命運
Do Not Destroy Your Own Destiny

吾說了又說，勸了又勸。千萬不要墮胎！千萬不要墮胎！

不要傻傻地以為沒有把孩子生出來，妳的生活會好過些。更不可以給這種理由，說那時候沒有錢，那時候還小，才 16 歲，18 歲，我害怕等等。

這麼多理由，當初為何還要縱慾呢？

妳天真地以為那麼簡單，哪知後來數十年糟糕了！整個樣子，整個命盤都變了。

墮胎等同於墮掉一切的福因啊！

吾真實看過太多太多這樣的例子了。請認真地思考再思考吾的勸告。

做男人的，不要始亂終棄、不負責任，以為魚水之歡不用付出代價。慫恿自己的女伴去墮胎，殺生之罪你一樣沒得幸免。

做母親的，對方不負責任，妳怎麼也象他一樣不負責任呢？不要讓恨的烏雲遮擋智慧的太陽。妳有最後的決定權。如果妳不要拿掉自己的孩子，沒有人可以逼妳走進那手術室，任由冷酷的醫療器材把嬰孩的身軀給砸碎，再吸出來丟棄。告訴妳，那血淋林的「肉碎」被丟進垃圾桶時，妳身後就會有位充滿恨意的水子靈（嬰靈），勢必要向父母復仇。

不要說妳走頭無路,妳應該知道會有那麼一天。到最後,妳要負起的因果報應,妳以為是吾在開玩笑嗎?妳真以為妳負得起嗎?別傻了!因果之事,不用妳、你信,一樣照報!

沒有能力養,可以讓別人領養,讓孩子的生命延續下去。

勸別人墮胎的人,很不忍心地告訴您,您自以為的一番好意早已種下惡因了。天底下沒有一位福神會跟隨像您這樣的幫兇。進行墮胎手術的醫護人員和做出和墮胎相關的產品和服務人士,後面的果報是妳、你得不償失的。妳、你的後代也會遭殃。

你以為吾在唬你?唬你根本得不到好處啊!

讓吾再說一次。吾所見過,墮過胎的婦女的業報有身患婦女病如子宮長瘤、婚姻不美滿、身體有異味、樣子比同輩老得快速、事業一波三折、得憂鬱症等。後來無法生育、流產、難產或生出不孝子女,很難帶、很難教因為是之前的水子靈來轉劫洩恨。

流產的、夭折的也被歸類為水子靈。父母親也得負起責任。因為吾觀現在很多婦女沒有照顧好身子,亂吃亂喝亂睡,卻一直想懷孕。結果受孕後,孩子在子宮不到十個星期就發現沒心跳,又或者生出體弱多病的孩子,導致夭折。這當中也參雜了前世的因因果果。吾批八字時,曾勸過一位婦女不要在某幾年懷孕。但她求子心切,不把吾的話放在心上,不斷嘗試受孕,結果胎死腹中三次之多。天啊!這都是殺生啊!

47

流產過、墮胎過或有夭折孩子的父母都得為孩子在寺廟安靈位、修法懺悔己業和報名超度法會至少 500 次（由有證量的上師主壇）。若有人說幾次就可以了，別聽信。自己用腦筋想想，如果吾用個鉗子夾碎您的頭直到頭破血流，再將您五馬分屍，血肉一團，再扔進垃圾桶，您會因為吾幾次的道歉賠償幾千元就原諒吾嗎？

　　吾已經做了十多年的師父，以上的所見所聞是確確實實的經驗。遇到有水子靈的婦女，彷彿是家常便飯。可見這草菅人命的問題事態嚴重。最令人擔憂的是很多女性對水子靈之事根本沒有悔意。寧願這樣子對待自己的親生骨肉，果然人比鬼更可怕！

──── 英譯 ────

I have said it over and over, and given countless advice on this.

Never go for an abortion! Never ever!

Do not foolishly think that by aborting the child, your life will be easier. It is absurd to hear reasons like "I am broke", "I am only 16 or 18, too young to have a child", "I am scared" etc.

So many excuses, then why did you allow yourself to fall

prey to the temptation of lust in the first place?

You were too naive to think that this is not a serious matter, but alas, years of sufferings will follow. Your entire destiny and well being will take a turn for the worst.

Aborting a baby is akin to aborting all seeds of fortune and merits!

I have truly seen too many, countless, in fact of such cases. Please ponder deeply upon my words of advice.

As a man, please be responsible and do not fool around, thinking that there is no price to pay for your reckless behaviour and casual flings. Persuading your female partner to go for abortion is the same as being an accomplice to a murder, for which the karmic retribution you shall not be spared either.

As the mother of the child, how could you shirk the responsibility, like your partner did? Do not let the dark cloud of hatred obstruct your light of wisdom. You hold the ultimate vote of decision. If you decide against abortion, no one can force you into the operating theater and allow the cold and feelingless medical instruments to crush the helpless fetus limp and sucking it out from your body. Let me tell you this, once the bloody and mangled piece of flesh, that was once your baby, is thrown into the waste bin, a fetal spirit will be standing right behind you, full of hatred for you and your partner. The spirit will be bent on exacting revenge on you and your partner. Please do not say that you had no other choice. You should know that this day will come. In the end, you would bear the karma of your cruel action. You think I am joking with you? You think you can easily bear this responsibility? Please do not be foolish. The Law of Karma holds its power over all, regardless if you believe it or not!

If you are not capable of raising the child, you can put the child up for fostering. At the very least, you preserve the child's life.

For those who had advised someone else to go for abortion, I really hate to tell you this, but your "kind" intention had already sowed the seed of sufferings for yourself in time to come. No god will bless an accomplice to such a heinous act. The same goes for other "accomplices" like the surgeons and nurses who administered the abortion, as well as those companies promoting abortion-related products and services. It is totally not worth it to bear the brunt of karma, and it will even implicate your descendants as well.

You think I am kidding you? I have absolutely nothing to gain from this!

Allow me to repeat myself. I have seen cases of women who had previous abortions and now suffering from various ailments concerning the female health (ovarian tumor, for example), their bodies giving off a strange odor, as well as a more aged appearance compared to their peers. They have depression bouts and their marriages encounter more obstacles. Any future pregnancy is either impossible or fraught with many difficulties resulting in miscarriages or traumatic births. The fetal spirit may reincarnate as their future offspring, who will turn out to be a child that is extremely difficult to teach and manage due to the innate hatred.

51

Babies that die from miscarriages or at a very young age after birth are classified under fetal spirits. The parents have to bear responsibility too. I have observed that many ladies do not take care of themselves well, wilfully consuming unhealthy food and adopting irregular sleeping hours, but yet hoping to bear a child. Once they get pregnant, the fetus can not sustain for more than ten weeks before being discovered that the child's heart has stopped. Should they carry the pregnancy to the full term and deliver the baby, the child, more often than not, will have a bad health predisposition, resulting in a premature death. In all that have happened, there are certainly past-life karmic retribution involved. I once advised a lady, who came to me for a birth chart analysis, not to try for a child during certain years. Overcame by desperation to have a child, my advice fell on deaf ears. As a result, she had to suffer a stillbirth, not once but thrice! My goodness, this is killing of another being!

For babies who died in abortions, miscarriages or at a young age after birth, the parents should set up a tablet in a suitable temple for the fetal spirit, cultivate repentance practice and enroll for bardo deliverance ceremonies (conducted by a Master with spiritual attainment) for the fetal spirit for at least five hundred times. Do not believe if somebody tell you that a few times is enough. Exercise your wisdom and think about this: If I use a pair of steel forceps and repeatedly crush your head and body, ripping you apart till you become a mangled state of flesh and blood before dumping you into a bin, will you forgive me just simply because I apologise a few times and compensate you with a few thousand dollars?

What I have described in this article are all true experiences from my line of work for the past ten over years. I have seen many ladies with previous abortions that it is becoming too common for my comfort. It is a very grave situation that human lives are treated as if they are not worth a straw. What worries me most is that many of these ladies have no sense of regret at all! To have no qualms in treating their

own flesh and blood with such cruelty, a human being can be more terrifying than a ghost indeed!

不懷好「孕」
Not Being Able To Conceive

　　凡夫俗子批八字，大多都離不開「妻、財、子、祿」。這四求中的「子」，就伸出不少令人啼笑皆非的真人真事來。在這人世間，「子女絕緣」對一般人而言，可謂人生一大憾事。因此，確實有人一擲千金，所謂「千處祈求」種種得子得女之方法。有些求有所得，有些卻不得要領。這是否有原由？玳瑚師父實實在在的告訴大家，天下間所發生的事情，皆有因緣因果，由不得你我信或不信。就好比肉眼看不到的細菌，妳、你不能否定它們的存在啊！因為到處都有細菌啊！

　　據吾所知及應證的，有無子女和「福德」是息息相關的，絕對和錢財無關係。就是因為如此，吾才苦口婆心勸了有又勸，說了又說，為的就是希望你們，能夠早日知道，「妻、財、子、祿」都是需要福德來「培植」。常做損人利己，還沒積德，就先缺德的人，是不會如願以償的。

　　很多很多人都想弄個「水落石出」，為何無法圓子女願？吾現在就為眾宣說，信不信由妳、你。其實就算妳、你不信，妳、你依然生存於因果內。不孕的原因：

一、墮過胎。殺生為五戒之首，罪之重可想而知。
二、犯淫。

三、家中爐位安錯。

四、臥床安錯。

五、神位安錯。

六、行商缺德。

七、誹謗修行人，以及佛菩薩。

八、答應神佛之事，卻遲遲未進行，且有意故犯，傲慢不可一世。

九、喜占人便宜。連修行人及佛菩薩都不放過，等等。

若妳、你誠心懺悔，再發願守戒行善布施，待罪消福增時，才能圓滿一切所求。

有首偈吾甚喜之，也常寫給有緣人。妳、你讀到這篇文章，也算與吾有緣，那就將這首偈披露於磁；

　　　　人心且莫把心欺，神鬼昭彰放過誰，
　　　　善惡到頭終有報，祇爭來早與來遲。

無論妳、你介不介意當不懷好「孕」之人，敗德之事千萬不可做，以免後悔莫及啊！

──── 英譯 ────

For many of us, the major reasons we get our birth chart analysed by a Master are none other than the following:

marriage, wealth, descendants and career. Out of these four reasons, the quest for descendants has spun many amusing real-life stories. In this human world, to have no luck with descendants is a shameful and regrettable fact for most of us. Thus there will be some who would spend fortunes to seek various ways for them to have children. Some got their wishes fulfilled, yet there were some whose hope crumbled in vain. Is there any reason for this? Let me tell you this, every thing that occurs in this world has its cause and affinity. It is not up to any of us to validate nor disbelieve this fact. It is akin to the bacteria that escape our naked eyes, yet we cannot deny their presence. Bacteria is everywhere!

According to what I know and have verified, the ability to have offspring is intricately connected to your merits. It has absolutely nothing to do with money. It is precisely so that I painstakingly remind everyone repeatedly to cultivate your merits so as to achieve good fortune in marriage, wealth, descendants and career. For those whose actions or thoughts bring harm to others, who destroy instead of accumulating your merits, your wishes in life would be hard to materialize.

Many people desperately want to know the reasons for them being childless. Here, I will expound the reasons. It is up to you to believe or not. As a matter of fact, the law of karma

(cause & effect) is quite oblivious to your acknowledgement of its existence. The several reasons for being childless:

1) Previous abortion(s), as it constitutes to killing. The most important precept in Buddhism is abstinence from killing so the severity of this sin when committed is obvious.
2) Sexual misconduct.
3) Wrong placement of the kitchen stove.
4) Wrong placement of the altar.
5) Wrong placement of the bed.
6) Lack of morals in conducting your business.
7) Defamation of the Buddhas, Bodhisattvas and Buddhist practitioners.
8) Willful breaking of your promise to the Buddhas and deities, deliberately delaying its execution due to arrogance.
9) Like to take advantage of others, including the Buddhas, Bodhisattvas and Buddhist practitioners
and so on.

If you are truly repentant and committed to uphold the precepts and lead a wholesome life (including doing kind deeds and giving to the needy), your negative karma will be reduced. Conversely, your merits will also increase, leading to the eventual fulfillment of your wishes.

There is a verse that I am particularly fond of, one which I often share with those whom I have affinity with. I believe that those of you reading this article also share an affinity with me. So I shall share the verse right here right now:

Do not think you can deceive your own heart.
Who have the omnipresent gods and ghosts ever let slip?
The good and the bad will get what they deserve in the end
It is just but a matter of time.

Regardless if you wish for a child or not, please do not commit unwholesome and immoral acts. You will live to regret it!

勿將生命來糟蹋
Do Not Trample on Your Life

　　貪駕快車是一種執著。明知是犯法,卻還是照做,就是一種人格的詆毀。如果真的撞到人,妳、你這一輩子不是要被囚嗎?就算不在牢房度過,妳、你的心也會被囚。

　　有位男士由他女兒帶到吾的面前,一副坐立難安,好幾天吃不下,睡不著的樣子。原來這位男士開車撞倒一位中學生,對方的家人要起訴他。女兒問吾是否能幫她爸爸。

　　一失足成千古恨,回頭已是百年身。這條路是一定回到妳、你的家,既然怎麼樣妳、你都會回到家,不需要乘一時之快啊!

　　吾真實替那位男士解決了這個大問題。但在這裡,要提醒諸位大德:或許妳、你所犯的過失,吾有能力為妳、你排憂解難,但這並不是做人的本質。做人一定要奉公守法,仁人愛物,己利而利人,己達而達人。做一位真正合乎人的人。

59

──── 英譯 ────────

The desire to drive at a high speed is a form of attachment. Transgressing the speed limit law wilfully shows the degeneration of a person's moral and character. If you knock down a person, you may end up paying for your recklessness with a lifetime behind bars. Even if you are spared from the jail, your heart will not be at ease.

There was this man whose daughter brought him to meet me, and I saw a man who was totally not at ease and had lost his appetite and sleep for the past few days. It turned out that he had knocked down a secondary school student while driving. As a result, the family of the student wanted to bring him to court. His daughter asked if I was able to help him out of this.

A wrong step can lead to a lifetime of regrets. Do not drive recklessly and speed for the sense of thrill or out of impatience. The route will lead you home eventually, so why speed unnecessarily?

True to my word, I have helped the man overcome this major problem. However here is a reminder for my dear readers: even though I may be able to help you get through the consequences of your misdeed safely, that should not be the way to live your life as a human. We must abide by the law, and show compassion to all men and beings. As in the Analects: To bring benefits to others as well, and not just for ourselves. To help others succeed when we have succeeded.

Be what a proper man ought to be.

天下本無事，庸人自擾之
Much Ado about Nothing

在聆聽一位女客人時，她說著說著就哭了。我問她怎麼了，她說：「壓力。」然後娓娓道出她壓力的各來源。

十多年來，這並非第一次有女客人在我面前落淚。男兒有淚不輕彈，曾有一位男客人因為婚姻問題，與我用餐時突然流淚。

其實天底下是沒有煩惱的，有煩惱也是眾生咎由自取，自做自受。

對於人生，不要什麼都要求最好的。如果你要學人家穿最流行的衣服、住最好的公寓、要賺很多錢、要重慾，你就是在為自己種了一個苦因，將來就得受這個苦果。

沒有這麼大的頭，不要戴這麼大的帽子。

人生的旅途中，要上坡下坡過橋，崎嶇的道路肯定有。

多去踏青，多看天空，學習天空的廣大，學習大地的包容。久而久之，心量會變大，如大自然一樣遼闊，無為而為。

「活著一天，感恩一天。活著一天，修行一天。活著一天，快樂一天。」每一天都是美好的一天！

可能您讀到這裡會覺得不用我說，您也懂。沒錯，這些三歲小孩都懂，但八十歲老翁卻做不到。

While listening attentively to a female client, she started crying as she spoke. I asked her what happened. She mumbled, "Stress." and told me about the various sources of stress in her life.

This is not the first time a female client cried in front of me, in my past ten years plus of consultation. Real men might not cry easily. A male client once cried halfway through our dinner because of marital problems.

Truth is, there is no affliction in this world. If there is, it is only because sentient beings ask for it and naturally have to bear the ill consequences of their own doings.

When it comes to life, do not keep wanting to have the best in everything. If you are going to be like most people, wanting to wear the most fashionable clothes, stay in the most upmarket condominium, earn lots of money and indulge in your desires, you are sowing a seed of suffering in your destiny and will have to experience its unpleasant fruit in the future.

To put it short, if you do not have a big head, do not wear such a large hat.

In the course of life, there is bound to be up slopes, down slopes and bridges to cross. The road is not going to be straight for sure.

Go spend more time with Nature, take time out to look at the sky and learn how expansive the sky is and how tolerant Mother Earth is. Over time, you are bound to have a broader mind that can stretch as vast as the nature.

For every day we are alive, be grateful.
For every day we are alive, cultivate.
For every day we are alive, be happy.
For everyday is a good day!

Perhaps after reading all this, you might think that all these are common sense and you know even without me saying it. Yes, you are right, even a three-year-old kid knows but yet an eighty-year-old man is still unable to do it.

心中有佛
Having The Buddha in Your Heart

很多人對於供佛菩薩神明有很錯的理念。現代人追求一切從簡。想供佛，求這個，求那個，卻又不要給祂這個，不要給祂那個。

有人說：「心中有佛就可以了！」

心中有佛，不是一般人可以講的。佛法是什麼，你都說不上來，如何心中有佛？你心中有佛，怎麼還會講別人是非呢？你心中有佛，怎麼還會有貪、嗔、痴、妒、慢、疑呢？怎麼沒有皈依，還阻止別人學佛向善呢？

更有人說：「神明應該比較大方一點，不要跟我們這些凡夫計較。」

為什麼神明就一定要比較大方？祂能成神，又不是因為你。你自己懶惰吝嗇，就不要怪罪在佛菩薩身上。記得，我們所做、所說、所想的一切都有鬼神在做記錄。

讓吾提醒你，佛菩薩沒有虧欠你。你身上所發生的事情，是你自己的業緣所感召。佛菩薩憐憫眾生的苦，才設方便法門，讓你能消業積福。佛菩薩根本不需要你那幾杯茶，那幾粒水果，祂們當然也不會和你計較。佛國天界所有的，遠遠遠遠超過我們人間。西方極樂世界可是金沙鋪地，隨便掉幾顆沙粒到人間，人看了呱呱大叫，叫價都已經是幾十千，幾十萬了。

　　家中的檀城代表了這家人的精神。檀城的旺度也決定了這家的興旺。每一個供品都有它的象徵意義。和「种瓜得瓜，种豆得豆」的道理一樣，你每天只供一杯清水，就想得到一家平安，有可能嗎？

　　有人自認很誠心，就隨意地自己動手清洗神像。這是非常無禮的行為。神的事宜要留給一個眞正的師父做。你身上有業障不清淨，不能去觸碰神像，況且，你也不懂得請神送神的儀軌，只是根據自己的心情亂做一通，毫無誠意可言。最令吾啼笑皆非的是，那位「誠心」人士還問吾能不能把家中的檀城給拆了，因為嫌麻煩。每天只供一杯水，還麻煩嗎？

65

　　已結婚的人，每天要懂得慰問伴侶：今天還好嗎？工作還可以嗎？吃飽了嗎？你把佛像請入家門，也是一樣。你可以將你的心事告訴佛菩薩，請祂們加持，但你也要懂得稱呼祂們、照顧祂們和關愛祂們。有戶家庭供奉的是阿彌陀佛，卻一直以為是釋迦摩尼佛，也有人把所有的菩薩都當作觀世音菩薩，有人教導時，又不肯學。這樣就叫心中有佛嗎？如果一直叫錯伴侶的名字又不肯買禮物給她、他，你說她、他會相信你心中有她、他嗎？

───── 英譯 ─────

Many people hold a misconception when it comes to

worshiping the Buddhas and Bodhisattvas. Modern-day people often go for simplicity. They scrimp on the offerings made yet wishing for the sky.

Some say, "It does not matter, as long as I have the Buddha in my heart."

Now, this is not something most people can say. What is the crux of Buddha's teachings? If you do not have a clue, how can the Buddha be in your heart? If you have the Buddha in your heart, why do you still talk behind people's back? Why would you still be afflicted with unwholesome traits of greed, anger, ignorance, jealousy, arrogance and doubt? If you have the Buddha in your heart, why have you not taken refuge in the Triple Gem? Why would you be discouraging others from learning the Dharma and walking the path of kindness?

Another person exclaimed to me, "The Gods should be more magnanimous and bear with us mortals!"

Why should the Gods be tolerant towards you? They ascended to the Heavens not because of you. Do not blame the Gods if you are the lazy and stingy one. Remember this, our every thought, word and action is recorded by the Gods, unseen to our naked eyes.

Let me remind you, the Buddha and Bodhisattvas owe you nothing. All that ever happened to you is a direct result of your own karmic manifestation. The Buddha and Bodhisattvas show their deep compassion to the sufferings of the sentient beings, by showing us the various ways to reduce your karmic afflictions and increase your merits. The Buddha and Bodhisattvas do not mind what your offerings are and certainly do not hanker after your meagre few cups of tea or that few pieces of fruits. These are nothing when compared to the Pure Land of Western Paradise, where the ground is paved with glittering gold and should only a few specks of the gold dust are to descend to our world, it will leave people in awe as we are talking about gold worth tens or hundreds of thousands.

The altar in a house has a huge bearing on the mental state of the occupants. The prosperity on show on the altar has a direct relation to that of the occupants. Every offering has its own symbolic essence. Just like you can only expect a watermelon when u plant a watermelon seed, why do you unrealistically expect blessings for yourself and your family when you only offer a miserable cup of plain water on your altar everyday? How would that be possible?

Some people think of themselves as devout and clean the statues of the Buddha and Bodhisattvas on their altar as and when they please. This is a very disrespectful action. Such activity should only be done by a virtuous Master of a high level of cultivation. You carry with you negative karma and in an impure state, you should not touch the statues in any way. Furthermore, with no formal knowledge of the consecration procedures, you are only conducting the rites based on your own thinking. That is a total lack of sincerity.

I was bemused when this "sincere" person came to ask me if she can dismantle her altar as she finds making a daily offering of water too tedious. How can offering only a cup of plain water daily be troublesome?

For those who are married, do you ask your spouse if he or she is doing well everyday? Or if he or she has had any issues at work? Or if he or she has eaten or not? If you have invited the Buddha and Bodhisattvas to your house, you must treat them the same. You can confide your woes in them and seek their blessings but you must also know how to address them formally, take care of them and love them. There is a family who, for many years, mistook the Amitabha Buddha statue in their altar as that of Shakyamuni Buddha. Yet another person thinks all Bodhisattva statues are the Guan Yin Bodhisattva and when corrected, he refuses to learn. How can such behaviour be having the Buddha in your heart? If you address your spouse by the wrong name or refuses to buy presents for him/her, do you think spouse will believe you when you say that he or she

lives in your heart?

你、妳的「欠影」
Your Shadow of Debt

出生於七、八十年代的讀者粉絲們，對這篇文章來說，應該是親切的。那是因為，本地有位女歌手，就在那個時期，唱了一首歌，名為「牽引」。而這首歌也成為她的成名曲。但吾所要傳達的，是「欠影」的種種，而並非「牽引」的種種。因此，讀者粉絲們可別搞錯了哦。哈哈哈！

吾以佛法與玄學等利益眾生，少說都有十多年了。特別是佛法所賦予吾的智慧，讓吾能夠漸漸成為「明眼人」，不被世俗虛幻的人與事，遮掩吾應盡畢生之精力，或許才能證得的無上智慧。只有如來無上智慧，才能堪破這世俗種種之假相不受六道無期徒刑之苦，而直取永恒真實的快樂和幸福。

有位少婦從網絡上得知有吾這位師父，固而來找吾為其新生寶寶撰名。後來是勘察陽宅地理，以及夫婦倆和他們第二位千金的名字，等等。在陽宅地理方面，他們的居家實在是很多「問題」的。但俗語說的好，「沒有三兩三，哪敢上梁山。」他們居家的「問題」，吾一一地為他們設法解決。唯獨一件事，吾實不相瞞地對他們說了又說，至今他們仍然沒有「行動」。因此，他們得賠上四個人的健康、事業、學業、財富、等等。更嚴重還會影響身理及心理。這些都是「巨大的損失」啊！

　　坦白說，吾大可領了紅包，揚長而去。可是，吾乃佛、道兼修的師父，怎可衹向錢看，而將戒律與誓願往後扔呢？後來吾從女方八字印證，原來是怨親債主討債來了，難怪屢勸「不改」。

　　怨親債主，不是衹有他們才有，其實普天下的人都有。輕者讓你，妳破財、傷心難過。重者與你，妳同歸於盡啊！或許有人會說：「哎喲！不用怕啦！來就跟他、她拼！」

　　玟瑚師父誠懇地告訴大家，我們是拼不過他們的。就算拼的過，也衹是等著下一世，或者來來世沒完沒了地纏來纏去而已，試問有何意義。更何況冤家宜解不宜結啊！八十年代有位女歌手叫千百惠的，不是唱過一首歌叫「癡癡纏」嗎？唱得好啊！何必癡癡纏呢？

71

　　吾寫這篇文章，是要提醒大家，且莫將怨親債主等閒視之，善惡到頭終有報，衹爭來早與來遲。他、她若在這一世與你、妳「相遇」，想過好日子，難啊！速速披露懺悔吧！速速積累更多善功德吧！再將所做的種種善功德，迴向怨親債主吧！祝願大家早日「甩掉」你們的「欠影」。哈哈哈！

—— 英譯 ——

For those of you who are born in the seventies and eighties, I am sure you would find the title of this article close to your heart. There was a local female singer from that era who rose to fame with the Chinese song "牽引", but this article is not about that song. Rather, the topic of this article "欠影" is similar sounding to the song. So please do not be confused.

For more than ten years, I have been using the Dharma and Chinese Metaphysics to benefit sentient beings. My wisdom has been greatly enhanced through the Dharma, enabling me to have a discerning eye and not be distracted by worldly delusions from my lifelong relentless pursuit of the Supreme Wisdom. Only with this Wisdom can we break through all aversions and endless sufferings in the six realms of existence, and achieve eternal joy and bliss.

A young married woman got to know me from the Internet and engaged my service to pen a name for her newborn. Geomancy audit of her house followed next, and lastly the name change of her husband, their second daughter and herself. Their house presented many Feng Shui problems but as the Chinese proverb goes, "One would not risk going up the mountains without courage." I resolved them all but there was one matter which I had repeatedly reminded them to do yet till today, no action was taken. This resulted in the decline of their health, wealth, academic results and careers. It would also affect their psychological health greatly. This are huge losses indeed!

I could have just walked away with my remuneration, but I

adhered to my precepts from my Dharma practice and did not allow monetary gain to motivate me. Upon reading her Bazi (birth chart), I realised her karmic debtors were hindering her. No wonder she refused to change her ways despite my reminders!

Karmic debtors are not just unique to this client of mine. In fact, every one of us has karmic debtors. For less serious cases, your karmic debtors will cause you to lose your wealth, emotional well-being etc. For the serious ones, it becomes a matter of life and death! Perhaps some of you might say, "There is no need to be afraid! I will fight them all!"

Here is a sincere advice from Master Dai Hu: there is no way to fight them all. Even if it seems that you have warded them off, that is only for this lifetime. They will be waiting for you in your next and future lifetimes to pester you persistently. Where is the meaning in this? Moreover, it is better to resolve enmity than to keep it alive. A female singer in the eighties by the name of Qian Bai Hui once sang a song titled Infatuated Entanglement. How true the lyrics are! Why the need for non-stop pestering?

I wrote this article to remind everyone not to take your karmic debtors lightly. The law of karma, be it good or bad, will catch up with you one day. You are going to have a tough time this life if you encounter your karmic debtors. Do your repentance quickly! Accumulate your merits swiftly! Dedicate all merits to your karmic debtors. I wish everyone to quickly dump your shadows of debt. Hahaha!

他、她的背影
His and Her Silhouettes

　　沒錯。這篇文章乃〈你、妳的「欠影」〉之延續。有這必要嗎？有的。爲甚麼有必要？一，反應熱烈。二，使人人明白，殺生所帶來的後患，何其大。三，救渡。

　　徒弟與學生的陪同下，在國外的購物商場選購服裝時，一位口齒伶俐，笑臉迎人的女服務員，嚮吾走來欲介紹一些服裝給吾時，除了她的「嬌」，吾更看見她的「背影」。說實在的，她的服務即快又熱情。可是她的「背影」，卻讓吾有那麼一點點的分心。她似乎有察覺到，臉部表情開始有點怪怪的。吾想應該是吾那時的表情，先讓她覺得怪怪的吧！

　　是這樣的，吾老早已看出未來精神的演變，以及她有「水子靈」的問題。吾說吾分心，是因爲吾乃修行人，更應該要慈、悲、喜、捨。正想著如何對她說。因此，無法「專心享受」她那殷勤的招待。後來吾決定將吾所見的，告知她對方。果然，她眞的有「水子靈」。吾就托吾之徒弟與學生，教導她如何處理這非同小可的過失，使大人和小孩都得到慰藉。

　　在一間英式酒店，等待欲前來給吾批八字大運的客人。一聲師父。吾抬頭一望，先望見的是一位女生。再來這女生就朝其右手邊，介紹說：「師父，這是我的男朋友。」這位

75

男生就是來批大運的主角。於是吾就朝左手邊望。呈現在吾眼前的，並不是這男生長得高頭大馬。而是這男生的習氣，以及他的「背影」。這男生到底有甚麼樣的「背影」？

當時吾所見的他的「背影」，是一團密密麻麻的黑影，類似昆蟲。後來我們談到殺生的話題時，他就道出曾有殺螞蟻及其他昆蟲的惡習。吾也認真地告訴他吾的所見，同時也讓他知道殺生的因果報應，更勸他不可任意、隨意殺生。

在第一義來說，殺人或殺昆蟲，都一樣的道理。罪重也不在話下。現在玬瑚師父就告訴你，妳們，有關殺嬰孩及殺昆蟲，所帶來的後患。所有墮胎的女性，頭髮容易掉、外表明顯衰老、皮膚快速老化、口及身體會有異味、未來定有忤逆之子、事業、家庭等等都不如意。殺昆蟲的，大多定有身疾或皮膚病、生石生瘤，等等。

千萬別以為玬瑚師父寫這些是唬你，妳們。絕對沒這雅興。這些全部都是千真萬確的。吾寫這篇文章的出發心，在文章的開頭已表明。吾也期盼大家能認知，因果報應實有，且屢報不爽啊！若您的身邊有這樣的人，快快介紹他，她觀讀這篇文章，功德一椿啊！〈她、他的「背影」〉，絕對沒王傑所唱的〈她的背影〉那樣簡單啊！

英譯

That is right. This article is a sequel to my previous one on the "Shadow of Debt". Is it necessary? It sure is! And for

the following reasons:

1) Great response to my previous article.
2) To let everyone knows the huge consequences of killing.
3) Salvation for sentient beings.

During an overseas trip, accompanied by my students, I went shopping for clothes and met this sales lady. She was smiley as she approached and had the gift of the gab. Beside her loveliness, I also saw the "silhouette" behind her. Frankly speaking, her service attitude was prompt and friendly, but I was slightly distracted by what I saw. She must have spotted my slight unease at that moment and looked at me oddly. I guess it must have been my own weird facial expression that prompted that.

Fact is, I saw the fetus spirit of the sales lady and how it will affect her mental health in the future. As a spiritual cultivator, we should all exercise compassion for all. I was distracted as I was thinking how to broach this issue with her. Finally, I decided to tell her what I saw. Indeed, she had indeed underwent abortion. I then instructed my students to convey to the sales lady the method to resolve this grave mistake of hers.

I was waiting for a client in a colonial-styled hotel to provide consultation on his life destiny (Bazi reading). I heard a greeting and looked up to see a lady. She gestured to her right and introduced, "Master, this is my boyfriend." The guy was the client I was waiting for. I saw, not his towering frame, but his energy and the silhouette behind him. What kind of silhouette was that?

At that moment, I saw a silhouette of densely packed black dots behind him. The black dots resembled small insects. In a later part of our conversation, he admitted that he used to have a habit of killing insects. I told him, seriously, what I saw and educated him on the bad karma of killing. I advised him not to wilfully take lives.

In the eye of the Ultimate Truth, killing a human being or an insect does not make a difference. It is a sin of similar huge proportion. Master Dai Hu shall tell you now the consequences of abortion and killing insects. Women who aborted their unborn child suffer from hair loss, look aged with fast aging skin, bad breath and body odour, insubordinate children and obstacles in their career and family. Killing of insects will results in bodily illness like skin disease, tumour growth etc.

Please do not think that Master Dai Hu is scaring you. I am definitely not in the mood for this now. All these are facts and I have stated my reasons at the beginning of this article. I look forward to everyone of you appreciating the law of cause and effect. Should u know anyone with the same

issues mentioned above, please get them to read this article. Consider it as a merit earned! Taiwanese singer Dave Wang sang a song with similar title, "她的背影", but that is just a mere proportion to what I have just shared!

向日
Looking Towards the Sun

　　游泳是吾超愛的運動，一個星期可游上三天。但每次欲出發前，定會探頭看一看，窗外天空是否豔陽高照，或是風和日麗，若兩者皆沒有，吾通常會打消出發的念頭，待隔天或隔幾天再說。吾喜見太陽公公，祇因太陽總給人光輝、振奮、希望、美好、愉悅，正面的能量是不在話下的。

　　很多人總以為，春天的花朵最嬌豔。其實春天是花綻放的季節，夏天是百花爭豔的季節。水果也是如此，祇要是陽光充足的地帶，水果特別香甜呢！別忘了哦！果王榴槤及果后山竹皆是熱帶國家的代表。說到花及水果，吾也開始「手舞足蹈」起來了。

　　其實不只花草樹木、蔬菜水果，人類及動物，甚至天下萬物，都倚賴日光能量，生存於這「動盪不安」的地球上。大日的「吸引力」是偉大、無私的，祂誰都普照，實無分別的普照。祂是我們所有學佛者應該學習的榜樣。就因如此，這些年來，吾較積極向日、觀日及學日，期盼早日能覺行圓滿，永斷輪迴之苦。

　　所謂向日是指朝正道，將妳、你的所能完全毫無保留地發揮與貢獻給所有的人類。觀日是讓永恆之光，正義之光引進自身的體內，並與之融合。學日則是希望能象太陽般破降黑暗，讓眾生永無恐懼，且能永在安穩。

吾實實在在地告訴大家，每天的觀日、向日及學日是非常非常必要的，只因大家都想一勞永逸啊！

Swimming is a sport I enjoy thoroughly, and I could do it up to three times a week. Every time before I set off for the pool, I would look out of the window and see if it is a sunny or a breezy day. If it is not that kind of weather, I would usually banish any thought of swimming that day and wait out for another day or two. I love to see Mr Sunshine, as He always gives people brilliance, excitement, hope, joy and all the positive energies.

81

Many people assume that the flowers are at their most brilliant in Spring time. In fact, Spring is when the flowers blossom, but Summer is when they compete to be the most radiant of them all. The same goes for fruits. As long as there is sufficient sunlight, the fruits harvested would be especially sweet! Do not forget that durian, the king of fruits, as well as mangosteen, the queen of fruits, are both grown in the tropics. I am dancing in delight as we are talking about fruits and flowers!

It is not just the plants and trees, vegetables and fruits. In fact, human beings and the animals, even all living beings in this world, rely heavily on the energy from the Sun to live on this tumultuous planet. The Sun wields a great and selfless influence, and shines on every one with no bias at all. We, as Buddhists, should learn from the great example set by the Sun. And this is the reason why, all these years, I have been looking up diligently to the Sun, observing and learning from the Sun, and looking forward to the day I attain Enlightenment and be eternally free from the sufferings of reincarnation.

What I meant by "looking towards the Sun" is to be on the Right Path, to make use of all your abilities and selflessly contribute to all of mankind. Observing the Sun is to channel the light of Eternity and Righteousness into our body and merge with it. Learning from the Sun is to emulate its ability to break through and vanquish all darkness, relieving all sentient beings of fear and giving them the serenity and stability they so crave for.

I am going to let everybody in on this: It is definitely a very important ritual to look towards the Sun, observe and learn from it every day because everybody is wishing for the one single shot of effort that can lead them to salvation!

在還沒變之前
Before The Change Unfolds

　　當年秦始皇因排儒，欲將所有的書焚盡，唯獨一本書他沒焚，究竟是哪一本書讓他「手下留情」呢？這本書是其身邊一位高官，仔細講解給他聽後，而得以「免於一死」。也唯有真實功德的書，才能繼續利益後世疾苦交加之眾生。這本書就是全世界，排名第一的《易經》。西方人把它稱為《The Book Of Changes》。

　　《易經》說明了一切都是在變化中，一切也無常態，暗合了佛所說的，一切皆無常啊！而這一切包含了天時、地理、人和，包含了六親眷屬之關係、人的身體、災難、情感、財富等等等，都在變化中。根本沒有一樣東西，我們可以將它留住，唯有藏在妳、你「心中最深處」的佛性，才是永恆不變的。所有的我們，欲想親見自己的佛性，一定要下苦功，真正實修佛法，持之以恆，最終才能親證你們原原本本的佛性，任運及自在。

　　從《易經》我們知道了，一切都在變，這是很好的。怎麼說呢？最起碼它已教會我們，不要去執著一切，應攝取當中的智慧，放開束縛，自在與快樂馬上奔向妳、你。這本《易經》實在讚！不說你們不知，五術山、醫、命、卜、相，皆出自於《易經》。若有人問妳、你，現在在做什麼啊？妳、你回應現在在研究算命，她、他應該不會有太大的

83

反應。但如果妳、你回應她、他，妳、你現在在研究《易經》，她、他的反應會是前所未有的。

　　玳瑚師父知曉天下本無事，庸人自擾也。在一切還沒變之前，何不認取這智慧，放下是解脫之門，想要快樂自在，這門是不二法門。

　　　　日落月昇又一天，野牛亂撞誰來牽；
　　　　不如研究此經典，任運自在樂無邊。

―――― 英譯 ――――

During the time of the Qin Dynasty, the Qin Emperor rejected the Teachings of Confucius and burnt all books, with the only exception of a single title. So which book was spared from the "burning death"? The virtues of this book was being extolled to the Emperor by a high-ranking official during that time and he convinced the Emperor not to burn this book. Only a book, with true merits and virtues, that can alleviate the sufferings of mankind, would be passed down centuries after centuries. This book, number one in the world, is non other than I Ching, or as named by the Westerners, The Book of Changes.

The Book of Changes states clearly that everything is in a constant flux of change and nothing is ever constant. This is aligned with the Buddha's teaching that nothing is

permanent! This includes the Heavens, Earth and Man, relationships with the family, one's health, disasters, emotions, wealth, etc. There is absolutely not a single thing we can hold on to forever, except your own Buddha Nature, buried deep in your heart. If you desire to see your own Buddha Nature, you must work hard and cultivate the Dharma. Only through relentless effort on this long journey, will you be able to finally realize your Buddha Nature and gain liberation.

We know from the Book of Changes that everything is constantly changing. This is a good thing. Why do I say that? Well, at least it teaches us to release all attachments and gain the wisdom from it. When you let go, joy and freedom will immediately find their way to you. This book is really praiseworthy! You may not know this but the five Chinese techniques of landform, medicine, destiny, divination and physiognomy stem from the Book of Changes. If someone is to ask you about your present occupation, and you answer that you are studying Destiny Analysis, the person probably might not show any big reaction. But if you tell that someone that you are doing research on the Book of Changes, you will be greeted with a reaction never seen before.

Master Dai Hu understands that nothing in this world actually matters, and it is only the ignorant who will bother himself with otherwise. Before any change unfolds, why not recognize this wisdom, detach and free yourself from this never-ending cycle? There is only one path to true happiness and freedom.

The sun sets, and the moon ascends.
Another day has gone by.
The wild cattle is in disarray with no one to shepherd them.
Why would you not delve into this treasure trove of a book?
And find yourself in everlasting bliss and freedom.

守護靈的正知
The Right Knowledge about Guardian Spirits

　　靈的世界並不是，也不可能三言兩語就訴說的完的。今天提筆寫這文章，主要原因有三。

一、很多很多人，道聽途說，以訛傳訛，造成人心惶惶，實爲過失，福德無增反減，這樣不算是智舉。

二、一知半解的情況，如何利己利他，冥陽兩利呢？

三、揭開守護靈的神秘面紗，一起修功德，向善也向上，皆大歡喜。

　　在學佛之前，吾對於靈是「敬而遠之」的。學佛及玄學昇做師父後，開始有機緣研究與接觸靈，才明白他們不爲人知的一面，也才從當初的「敬而遠之」，到今日的「敬而近之」。所以吾才知曉，原來他們比人更眞，與他們交友，並不需要家財萬貫、居住豪宅、出入名車，等等。他們是交心，而不交金。他們有恩必報的，不像人如此受恩，卻反過來恩將仇報。

　　据吾所知，守護靈有些是過世的祖父或祖母、過世的父親或母親、過世的親朋戚友、過世的兄弟姐妹、過世的好朋友、過世的丈夫或妻子、過世的孩子，等等。無論如何，玳瑚師父在此必須提醒你們，這些守護靈們，是時時在你們左

右的，他們會因為你們的不正念頭及行為，生起瞋念而墮落三惡道。千萬不可無知地以為；好囉！不用拜囉！告訴你們，他們若墮落，你們在現實生活中，將失去守護力，而不好的靈馬上就來附在你們的身上或身中，從此「暗無天日」，你們死後，也同樣地墮落三惡道。智慧與愚痴，可見一般。

　　平時應該多多注意自己的起心動念、言談舉止、修善修福，這樣的善心與孝心才能夠讓我們的守護靈昇格，他們一昇格，我們在陽世間自然就昇格，無須東拜西拜南拜北拜，又或者亂亂拜，最終落入迷信幫，那就不太好。不如做位守護靈的正知者吧！日吉祥，夜吉祥，天天皆吉祥。

─── 英譯 ───

The realm of spirits cannot be fully explained in a mere two or three sentences. I wrote this article today for three main reasons.

1. Many people formed inaccurate pictures of the spiritual realm from hearsay. This created confusion and irrational fear through spreading of incorrect information, resulting in loss of merits. Such negligence is an unwise thing to do.

2. With only superficial knowledge, how can we benefit ourselves and others, both the living and the dead?

3. By lifting the veil of secrecy on our guardian spirits, we can all cultivate more merits and kindness with a more positive outlook and attain mutual happiness for everyone.

Before I became a Buddhist, I have due respect for the spiritual realm, but I kept a respectful distance away from them. After my exposure to the Dharma and metaphysics, and becoming a Master in my own right, the affinity with them drew closer and I had the opportunity to understand the unknown side of them through various interactions. This newfound knowledge and respect drew me closer to the spiritual realm. I have discovered that the nature of the spiritual beings is more sincere than humans. The spiritual beings do not need wealth, luxurious houses and branded cars etc, in order to befriend them. They do not talk money, and their sincerity stems from their hearts. They remember kindness and will seek to repay them, unlike some humans who often bite the hand that feeds them.

To my knowledge, our spiritual guardians may well be our family relations who have passed away-our late grandparents, parents, siblings, spouses, children, relatives or good friends etc. Regardless of who they might be, let me remind everyone that these spiritual guardians are always by your side. They will be affected by your non-virtuous thoughts or actions, which will cause hatred and anger to arise in them, and consequently cause them to fall into the three lower realms of existence. Please do not be ignorant and think that you would be rid of them this way and say hurray to not having to make prayers to them. The truth is, should they fall into the lower realms, you will lose their protection, allowing other undesirable spirits to come unto you. Your life will be shrouded in darkness and when you pass on, you will plunge into the lower realms as well. There is a thin line between wisdom and ignorance.

In our daily moments, we ought to be very aware of the thoughts and intentions arising from our mind, and the consequential action and speech. We must consciously cultivate merits and kindness. In this way, our virtues and filial piety will enable our spiritual guardians to rise in rank. Once our spiritual guardians assume greater power, our lives in this world would naturally improve as well. There is absolutely no need to pray at every other place mindlessly, and eventually join the bandwagon of superstition. Let's have the correct and positive knowledge when it comes to our spiritual guardians.

I wish everyone an auspicious day, auspicious night and auspiciousness every single day!

有拜有保佑
Blessings For The Ones Who Pray

今天，正月初九，是天公誕，就是玉皇大天尊的聖誕，也就是我們華人在家所供奉的「天官賜福」也。那為什麼要在這天講天公誕，有什麼特別需要在這天講呢？

是這樣的，因為當偉大的聖者，佛陀，在菩提樹下成道之時，祂原本就想隨即進入涅槃，沒有想要住世傳達佛法。祂認為世間的人不會明白祂的證悟。這時候就有兩位大天神下降，其中一位就是，在佛家譽為帝釋天主，的玉皇大天尊。另外一位就是大梵天王。祂們雙雙下降，很客氣、很殷勤、很誠懇地請佛住世。

如果當年沒有玉皇大天尊佛住世，我們所有的人類到現在都還不會有出離這六道輪迴的一個法門，所以祂實為我們眾生的大恩人。因此在祂的聖誕，我們不能夠忘記，必須得感恩圖報。在這時候，一般的福建人就會買長長的甘蔗。在天公誕的那一天，供上非常珍貴的珍品來供養玉皇大天尊。我也希望所有的華族同胞，家中沒有安天公爐的，在家可以自行準備一個長長、乾淨的桌子，又拿個乾淨的水果罐的空罐子，外圍用紅紙包著，寫上「天官賜福」，放八分米，插三支大香，和一包小香供給家庭成員，各持三支香，為自己的所需祝禱。

最主要是這一天是我們很好向祂，南無天公玉皇大天

91

尊，致謝的一天。在祂的聖誕來臨之前，這世面上就會出現一種水果叫「佛手」。我們理應買這「佛手」在天公誕供養祂。祂等同於皇帝，可是比皇帝更尊貴，因爲人間的皇帝也必須祂點名才能夠做地上的皇帝。

　　祂是我們眾生的父親和大恩人。這一天真的很值得我們上供祂、誦經持咒、向祂懺悔我們日常生活中所犯的種種大小過失及罪，祈求祂放光地加持我們業障消除、身心身體健康、家庭圓滿、事業順心等等等。天公是古佛再來，因此，在祂的佛辰懺悔絕對可以消業障。祝福你們。

Today is the Ninth Day of the First Lunar Month, which coincides with the auspicious Birthday of the Heavenly Jade Emperor, or "Tian Gong Dan". Why would I talk about this auspicious event? What is the significance of this day?

The significance of it is as follows: When the Great Gautama Buddha, also known as Shakyamuni Buddha, achieved Enlightenment under the Bodhi Tree, the Buddha had wanted to enter Nirvana and not remain in the human realm. He felt that the mortals would not understand His wisdom and attainment. At that very moment, two heavenly beings descended from the Heavens. One of them is the Heavenly Jade Emperor, the other one the Great Lord

Brahma. They respectfully, diligently and sincerely persuaded the Buddha to remain in the mortal realm to propagate the Dharma.

If the Heavenly Jade Emperor did not convince the Buddha to remain in this realm, we mortals would never have a way to escape from the six realms of existence, thus He is regarded as the Great Benefactor of all sentient beings. That is why on His birthday, we must not forget and must repay this gratitude. During this day, Chinese people of Hokkien descent would buy long sugar canes as an offering to the Heavenly Emperor, together with other precious offerings. I hope that for those of us Chinese who do not worship the Heavenly Jade Emperor at home, you can prepare a long, clean table, and a empty tin can that was used to contain fruits. Wrap a red paper outside the can and write in Chinese characters "天官賜福" (Blessings from Heavenly Emperor) on it. Fill up 80% of the can with rice grains, and plant 3 big joss sticks, as well as prepare a small pack of joss sticks for the whole family. Each family member can each hold 3 small joss sticks and say their own prayers.

Most importantly, it is an auspicious day to pay our respects and gratitude to Him, the Heavenly Emperor. During this period, you may see a unique kind of fruit known as "Buddha Hand". We should buy this fruit as an offering to Him. His stature is as noble as an Emperor and even more esteemed. Even the mortal kings in our world are also anointed by Him.

The Heavenly Emperor is like the Father and Benefactor of all sentient beings. This day, the Ninth Day of the First Lunar Month, is indeed worthwhile and significant to present our offerings, to recite sutras and chant the mantras and to seek repentance for all sins we have committed in our daily lives. We can also pray for His Light and Blessings to remove our karmic hindrances, to enable us to have good physical and mental health, to have good family ties, and a fulfilling career, etc. The Heavenly Jade Emperor is a reincarnation of an ancient Buddha, thus on this auspicious day, you can definitely seek repentance and blessings from Him. Here's sending my best wishes to you.

占便宜的未來循環
Taking Advantage Of Others & Its Repercussion

　　吾在還沒得到「智慧」之前，並未認證思考過，有關占他人便宜，會有怎麼樣的「循環」。一直到吾當了師父，才漸漸開始觀照，占他人便宜的人，其後來的「循環」。

　　多年的觀照下，喜占他人便宜的人，為數還真不少。就因如此，吾有必要讓你們，正式瞭解占他人便宜，未來的「循環」將會是怎麼樣的。

　　喜占他人便宜的人，有以下三種：
　　（一）多世或前世習氣。
　　（二）慳貪之人。
　　（三）明知故犯。

　　無論妳、你是屬哪一種，終究非善行。非善行，那就是惡行了哦！惡行是會有惡報的。在現實生活中，這種錯誤理念及行為，將會傳給你們未來的下一代，因基因之故。妳、你本身受惡報，難道妳、你也想妳、你的子女，以及孫輩們全部都受惡報嗎？其實那是不只的，我們所有的起心動念、言談舉止，或多或少，也會影響我們祖先們的「昇降」問題。慎之，慎之。

　　因果乃維護宇宙間的平衡，正如種瓜得瓜，種豆得豆，

分毫不差也。占人便宜，等同享他人之福也。占得越多，不要以為得到越多，其實妳、你的福份，相對的在扣除，等妳、你的福份，完全被扣除了之後，不如意及不幸的事情，就會馬上演化在妳、你身上，而另一邊，妳、你也有欠於對方，將來的「循環」，就是得為對方「做牛做馬」。看來女傭介紹公司，應該會很有市場。哈！哈！哈！

因緣果報就是如此地鮮明，這樣才叫公平，這樣才能讓人信服。常言道：不是不報，是時辰未到。

施主一粒米，大似須彌山，
倘若無功德，披毛戴角還。

──── 英譯 ────

Before I gain wisdom from the Dharma, I did not give any serious thought about the consequences and vicious cycle of taking advantage of others. Only until I became a Master that I slowly realized the ills and future repercussion of this act.

After years of illuminated observation, I come to the conclusion that there are indeed many people who like to take advantage of others. Thus I see the need to let you really understand its vicious cycle.

There are generally three kinds of people who like to take advantage of others:

1. Those who already have this bad habit for the past many lives.

2. Those who have an insatiable greed.

3. Those who wilfully transgress.

Whichever category you belong to does not do you any good as this act is not of merit, but of harm, thereby culminating negative karma. In the reality of life today, this harmful thinking and behavior will be perpetuated by your descendants, due to reason of genetics. Do you wish for your descendants to suffer the same fate and consequences that you do? In actual fact, there is actually more to it. Our every thought, word and action invariably has an effect on our ancestors, determining if they ascend to the bliss of Heavens or fall into the abyss of Hell. Beware, beware!

The Law of Karma is the great equalizer and it ensures balance in this Universe. Using the simple analogy: if you plant the seed of a melon, you will get melon during harvest. Likewise, you would harvest peas if you had sow their seeds earlier on. Taking advantage of another is akin to enjoying merits that does not belong to you. Do not think that the more you get, the more you will enjoy. In reality, your own merit is being deducted as you take advantage of others. And when your own merits run out, you will start to experience obstacles and misfortunes in your life. As you take advantage of another, you will owe that person a debt. When payback time comes along in the future lives, you will find yourself working like a slave for that very person you were indebted to in the past. Well, it seems like the maid agencies will be enjoying brisk business! Ha ha ha!

The Law of Karma (Cause and Effect) is indeed clear and definitely impartial, hence our conviction in it is absolute. As the saying goes, "Retribution is only a matter of Time. "

A Grain of Rice from the Benefactor,
Is as Vast as the Sumeru,
Should you think that is of no merit,
In a fur coat and with horns,
You will be paying back.

佛在心頭坐
The Buddha Sits In My Heart

　　吾想吾的讀者粉絲們應該有看過由游本昌主演的《濟公》，這部電視劇的主題曲膾炙人口，裡面唱到：「酒肉穿腸過」，「佛祖在心頭坐」。

　　如何確定佛在你心頭坐？

　　你時時刻刻的起心動念，舉手投足都是在善的，都是在戒律中，沒有跟道德理念有衝突，沒有占人家便宜。

　　佛沒有喜歡或不喜歡。你看到你討厭的人，已經沒有起瞋念。你看所有的人都能把他們當成佛。

　　如果你沒有，你怎麼說心中有佛？心中有佛的人會謙虛。

　　你去參加公司的常年晚宴，因為社交，而喝酒。你把酒喝下去，沒有讓酒煽動你的心。

　　你吃肉，能不把肉當成肉，你懂得持咒超度畜靈，你懂得供養，沒有貪口腹之欲。

　　如果你不能，你怎麼說酒肉穿腸過？

　　曾在吾根本上師蓮生活佛書中讀到：

　　在宋孝宗的時代，有位叫「戒闍黎」的大行者，祂的食量很大，聽說能吃三個豬頭、五斗酒。

　　有位汪平甫的太守，請戒闍黎來吃飯。

　　戒闍黎又是酒，又是肉，吃得不亦樂乎，果然食量大的

驚人，廿人份的，一口氣全吃光，如同秋風掃落葉。

　　戒闍黎到了汪太守的後院，汪太守夫人偷偷瞧見，只見戒闍黎口中吐出酒箭，空中有鬼神接去。

　　又吐出肉，空中又有鬼神接去。

　　太守夫人告訴太守，汪太守十分驚駭，從此對這位戒闍黎，敬畏得五體投地，也皈依了戒闍黎。

　　舉此例說明，戒闍黎表面上喝酒吃肉，其實他根本沒有，真正是「酒肉穿腸過」。（傳說中的戒闍黎是文殊菩薩的化身。）

　　你說佛在你心頭坐，請問：

　　你是皈依的佛弟子嗎？
　　你有日日參禪修法嗎？
　　你有日日研讀佛法嗎？
　　你有日日渡眾生嗎？
　　你有日日菩提精進嗎？

　　如果你沒有，請不要說你心中有佛因為這是妄語。不要在佛菩薩面前裝無知，拿佛菩薩來妄語及誤導他人會自食其果。

　　酒肉穿腸過，佛在心頭坐，聽起來很簡單，三歲小孩雖懂但八十歲老翁做不到。

I am guessing most of my readers and fans would have seen the Chinese drama serial "Ji Gong", starring Chinese actor You Benchang. The popular theme song has lyrics going like this, "Wine & meat pass through the intestines", "The Buddha sits in my heart".

How can you be sure that the Buddha is in your heart?

In each moment of your life, every emotion and thought you have, every action you do, stems from kindness and is in accordance with the precepts. There is no conflict with the morals and ethics and there is no taking advantage of another sentient being.

The Buddha does not feel any affection or hatred. When you see someone you dislike, does hatred arise in you? Do you treat all other sentient beings, even the animals and ghosts, as Buddhas?

If you are not able to do so, how could you say that the Buddha resides in your heart? A person who truly has the Buddha in his heart practices humility.

When you attend your company's Dinner and Dance event,

and consume alcohol for social reasons, the alcohol will not fan the flames and desires of your heart.

When you devour meat, you do not see it as meat. You possess the knowledge to deliver the spirit of the animal through mantra recitation. You know how to make an offering and no greed for food and alcohol arise in you.

If you cannot do all of the above, how could you say that "wine and meat only pass through the intestines"?

From a writing by my Root Guru, Living Buddha Lian Sheng, I read of this:

During the Song Dynasty, there lived a powerful spiritual cultivator by the name of Precept Master. He was known for his ferocious appetite and word had it that He could easily polish off three pigs and quaff five jars of wine.

Wang Ping Pu, a local governor, invited the Precept Master to his home for a meal.

The appetite of Precepts Master was indeed a sight to behold. He happily devoured meat and wine, enough to feed over twenty people, as speedily as the autumn winds sweeping away the fallen leaves.

After the meal, the Precept Master went to the backyard, with the wife of the governor secretly watching him by the side. She saw the Precept Master opened His mouth and arrows of meat and wine shot through the air, into the waiting arms of the spirits and gods!

She told the governor what she witnessed and from that moment onwards, he was in awe and veneration of the Precept Master and took refuge under Him.

This story tells us that even though the Precept Master was seen physically consuming the meat and wine, he was not. This is the true essence of "wine and meat only pass through the intestines".

Legend had it that this Precept Master is a manifestation of the Manjusri Bodhisattva.

You proclaim that the Buddha sits in your heart, but let me ask you:

Have you taken refuge in the Triple Gem?
Do you practice insightful meditation and cultivate everyday?
Do you study the Dharma deeply everyday?
Do you help other sentient beings by expounding the Dharma to them everyday?

Do you diligently strive towards Enlightenment everyday?

If you do not, please do not say that you have the Buddha in your heart because that is an outright lie. Do not act ignorant in front of the Buddhas and Bodhisattvas, as there is a heavy price to pay for sprouting untruth to Them and using Them to mislead others.

"Wine and meat only pass through the intestines, the Buddha sits in my heart". This verse is simple to the ears, simple for a three-year-old to know but extremely challenging for a eighty-year-old man to fulfill.

你不要的那個小孩還在
The Baby You Did Not Want Is Still Around

上個星期一，我到台中的新光三越買褲。在臺灣買褲一大好處是櫃檯專賣店都提供即刻改褲的服務。等待當兒，我向售貨員要了一張白紙，免費為她測名。

離開前，我問：「你有曾經不要過孩子嗎？」

她一臉驚訝地點了點頭說有。

「你要為你的孩子報名超度。他一直還在你的身邊走來走去。」

我不只看到售貨員的嬰靈，也稱為水子靈，更看到她未來精神的問題。我看人不是單純地看外貌，而是看進去裡面，看他的氣色、他的磁場、他的思維。

我看到很多女客人身邊有水子靈，但她們絲毫沒有悔意，可見這問題很大，需要多去告訴人們水子靈會帶來的問題。

很多人對「失去」的孩子都漠不關心。世人無知，不知蓄意墮胎，先影響到個人，然後家庭、社會，之後就是國家。很多家庭的風波如孩子叛逆、事業不振、生意衰敗、疾病纏身、夫妻失和，就是因為沒有人去留意這些被遺忘的孩子。等到事情發生時，才去求神拜佛。其實真正要求的是自己。

在這宇宙間，根本沒有一個人有權利剝奪另外一個人的生命，或一個生物，就算肉眼看不到的細菌，這些都是不能

夠的，更何況是一個比較具有靈性的人。眾生皆有佛性，墮胎如殺佛。五戒裡面，殺生為第一重罪，所以妻財子祿這些福都會在頓時間被消除很多很多，如一粒蘋果在分秒中被切成一半，所以不可不慎。

很多人以為經過人工墮胎，孩子就不會出現在她們的生命里。告訴你，你的想法是錯，錯，錯。被打掉的孩子會以另外一個形體留在你的身邊，因為你還欠他，而這個欠是多了一倍，甚至多好幾倍。你下一個生出來的孩子，為什麼會是體弱多病、軟骨、有唐氏綜合症或很難教，多方面地耗盡你的體力、家產和精神，不是沒有原因啊！

被殺的孩子最想看到我們誠懇地懺悔跟向他道歉，再求真正有證量的法師或修行人為水子靈做超度法事。這樣雙方之間才能夠解掉那個冤，否則未來一定是悲慘的。我看到我的女客人，因為水子靈的問題，身體有異味、脫髮、睡不好、健康每況愈下、甚至有婦女健康和精神問題。就算當初是男伴要求墮胎，女的責任始終比較多因為她是做出最終決定的人。

我們都要快樂輕鬆地過日子，曾幾何時卻增加了自己的負擔？所以大家要動動腦筋，不要一失足成千古恨。

―――― 英譯 ――――――――――――

Last Monday, I was buying a pair of pants at the Shin Kong Mitsukoshi department store in Taichung. The good thing

about buying pants in Taiwan is the on-the-spot alteration service they provide. While waiting for the alteration, I asked for a piece of paper from the sales lady and gave her a free Name Analysis.

Before leaving, I asked, "Have you not want a child before?"

She nodded yes, with a bewildered look on her face.

"The spirit of your child is still lingering around you. You need to enroll in puja sessions to deliver his spirit to a better realm.

What I saw was not just the fetus spirit, I also saw the emotional ailments that would take place in the sales lady in time to come. When I look at a person, I see beyond the outer appearance and read into their energy fields and mental thoughts. "

A lot of my female clients have fetus spirits with them from their past abortions but scarily, they have little regret. This is a serious matter that needs a much broader awareness on the implications of abortions.

Many people are not concerned about their aborted babies. A great majority of us are ignorant about the grave effect of deliberate abortion, from oneself to the other family members, even affecting our society and country on the whole. Family problems like difficult children, flagging careers, failing businesses, illnesses and broken marriages are caused by our neglect of these fetus spirits. It is not too late to repent now.

In this universe, no one has the right to take away the life of another person, another animal and even the micro-organisms which escape our naked eyes. There exists a Buddha nature in all living beings. To abort a child is akin to killing a Buddha. I sincerely hope all of us will meet enlightened ones in our life to guide us onto the path of light.

Amongst the five precepts of Buddhism, the act of killing carries the most severity, heavily and speedily reducing our fortunes in marriage, wealth, descendants, career and health. It is akin to halving an apple in a split second, thus we need to be very cautious against committing the act of killing.

Many who had an abortion perceived that their child would not appear in their lives again. How wrong you are! Their aborted fetus spirits will manifest in other forms, as their karmic debtors. The next child that comes along is likely to be sickly or very hard to teach, draining the energy and resources of the parents. This is the law of karma!

The aborted children seek a sincere apology from their parents and a true cultivator with the ability to do deliverance pujas for them. It is only through sincere repentance that the enmity and grievances in the spirits of the aborted children can be resolved. Misfortune befalls those who chose otherwise. Many of my female clients with past abortions suffered from various ailments: strange body odor, hair loss, poor sleep, women health issues and even declining mental health. Even though the man might have initiated, the woman is ultimately the final decision maker when it comes to abortion and thus bears a larger responsibility.

Everyone yearns for an easy, carefree life, but why are we adding burdens to ourselves? Let's think harder about this for one wrong step may cause a lifelong of regret.

你知道「我」在等你嗎？
Do You Know "I" am Waiting For You?

　　近日的出差，到一位患有重病的年青人住處，勘察其陽宅風水。在其門外打開羅盤看坐山向首時，他快速地稱呼吾，並開門迎接吾及吾的徒弟學生們。吾當然也禮貌地抬頭回禮，可是吾的看見，不只是這位年輕人而已，吾更看見其身上的「業印」。

　　親愛的諸位大德，妳、你們可曾記得，吾之前的作品，〈妳、你的「欠」影〉及〈他、她的「背」影〉呢？有些人的怨親債主及纏身業靈比較少，其家庭、健康、事業、感情、生意等各方面的問題、就沒什麼問題，或較遲才出問題。有些怨親債主，及纏身業靈多的，其各方面定較早出問題。正所謂，善惡到頭終有報，祇爭來早與來遲。

　　看了這位年青人的陽宅風水後，吾和徒弟及學生們，馬不停蹄地飛奔市區，趕赴一對學生夫婦的飯局。飯局後，吾親自為他們挑選幾件能為他們「遮雨擋風」的衣服。佛說無常迅速。吾細心為他們挑選的這些「擋風遮雨」的衣服，是希望吾不在他們的身邊時，她他們可以平安吉祥。

　　原本健康、快樂、如意的我們，不應該得意忘形。反而應該趁我們「盛狀」的時候，快快懺悔己過、行善布施、積累更厚的福報，以備「急時之需」。千萬不要以為我們永遠都會好，也千萬不要常想常說，心好就好。如果心好，為何

又推拒與人為善呢？如果心好，又為何常「情緒不穩」呢？如果心好，又為何常占人便宜呢？如果心好，又為何常黑白講，顛倒是非呢？如果心好，又為何不為妳、你過去世及現世、所對不起的及傷害過的人與事，道歉、懺悔及謀求福利呢？她、他、牠們一直都在等妳、你，妳、你可知道嗎？

On a recent Feng Shui audit assignment, I visited the residence of a young man stricken with a serious illness. While I stood outside his main door, taking readings of the sitting and facing directions with my Luo Pan (Chinese compass), he swiftly greeted me and opened the door to welcome my students and I. Of course, I politely raised my head to reciprocate. But what I saw was not just a young man, I saw the marks of karma on him.

My beloved readers, do you remember two of my previous articles titled "Your Shadow of Debt" and "His and Her Silhouettes"? Some people have lesser karmic debtors, thus their family, health, career, relationships, business and other aspects of their life have little obstacles now or that the occurrence of these obstacles has been delayed. On the other hand, those people with many karmic debtors will experience countless obstacles in all aspects of their life from a young age. As the saying goes, "The good and the bad will reap their just rewards at the end. It is only a matter of which comes first. "

After I have completed the Feng Shui audit for this young man, my students and I immediately made our way to town to attend a dinner appointment with another student couple. After the meal, I personally picked a few clothing items that would give them protection from life's harsh weathers. The Buddha expounded the fleeting impermanence of life, that changes are always speedy. I painstakingly selected the clothing items for them in hope that they will still be safe when I am not by their sides.

We should not be complacent in times of good fortune, good health and happiness. Instead, we should realise that we are now in a prime position to quickly repent for our past misdeeds, give generously to others, and accumulate more merits to buffer us when the time of crisis arrives. Do not be deluded that the good times will last forever. Nor should you think or say that as long as you have a good heart, so will your life. If you have a good heart, why do you refuse to perform good deeds? If you have a good heart, why are you often emotionally unstable? If you have a good heart, why do you frequently take advantage of others? If you have a good heart, why do you twist and contort the facts? If you have a good heart, why will you not repent your misdeeds to those people whom you hurt from your present

and past lifetimes, and seek blessings for them?.

Are you totally clueless that "they" have been waiting for you all these while?

我是妳、你最好的朋友
I am Your Best Friend

　　打從年少就已見聞許多「感人肺腑」、「可歌可泣」的人與事。就在那個時候，內心深處很自然的，有了這麼一個打算，願吾擁有「非一般的能力」，能夠解決一切眾生的問題，同時也能給予他們快樂、給予他們希望、給予他們方向、給予他們知識、開啟他們的智慧，讓他們能夠永遠離苦得樂。

　　「打算」歸「打算」。吾也有自己的「業緣」要還。一路來，還得非常非常不容易。幸好這一世吾依然能夠皈依真正的明師，學習真正的佛法，得以業消福增、智慧增長，腦筋越來越清醒，眼睛越來越「明亮」，觀破煩惱，直取真正的幸福與快樂。要不然就沒有玳瑚師父了。因此，吾不能不感恩吾的皈依師父，以及冥冥中大力加持和守護吾的佛菩薩、歷代傳承祖師們、所有的金剛護法、諸天及龍天護法們。

　　「雨過天晴」後，吾並沒有就此「享受人生」。反而比以前更精進。因為，吾的內心深處，仍然有幾個字亮光著。那就是：佛法與玄學，同步利益眾生。就因這誓願，人們在睡，吾則在用功。人們在玩樂，吾也在用功。吾不是不懂得「善待」自己，吾是希望做個有信用的人啊！

　　學佛的人，都得懂得「諸法因緣生，諸法因緣滅」。倘

若妳、你不懂得，衹好待妳、你我有緣見面時，才為妳、你開示。人生不如意十之八九，而當中也有它的因跟果。若是有一天，這些不如意的事情困擾著妳、你，身邊無人給予妳、你援助，千萬不可就「這麼一走了之」（自殺），趕快撥號電話給吾，若吾沒接，請傳短訊或留言。記住，記住，無論妳、你是健不健全，美或丑，富或貧，胖或瘦，甚至妳、你的快樂和悲傷吾都要，衹因「我是妳、你的最好的朋友」。

───── 英譯 ─────

Since young, I have witnessed many heart-breaking and tear-jerking episodes of life stories. Deep inside me, a vision naturally arose: May I possess extraordinary powers to solve the problems of all sentient beings, and at the same time, give them joy, hope, direction, knowledge and wisdom. I want to guide them to bliss, and away from all sufferings.

It is one thing to plan and another to actualise it. I have my fair share of karmic debts to repay. It has been an extremely tough journey thus far. Thankfully, in this lifetime, I am still able to seek refuge in an enlightened Guru and learn the Dharma to negate my negative karma and increase my merits and wisdom. I have achieved a deep clarity, breaking free of mental defilements and directly achieve true happiness. Without all these, there would be no Master Dai Hu today. Thus I cannot but be grateful to my Guru Master as well as the blessings and empowerments from the Buddhas, Bodhisattvas, past linage gurus and all Dharma Protectors.

Now that the "rainy days" are over, I did not rest on my laurels but instead strive harder. All for the promise that I will use the Dharma and Chinese Metaphysics to benefit all sentient beings. I work diligently when others are asleep. I pressed on painstakingly while others are having fun. It is not a lack of self-love, but I want to be a person true to my promise right till the end!

All Buddhists should know the phenomena of dependent origination. If you are unfamiliar with this principle, let me explain to you when we have the affinity to meet. In life, things do not always work out the way we want and every thing that happens has its own cause and effect. Should you, one day, be so troubled by your setbacks in life and there is no one by your side to aid you, please do not seek to end your life. Quickly give me a call. Drop me a text or voice message if your call is not answered. Whether you are able-bodied or disabled, whether you are good-looking or ugly, whether you are rich or poor, whether you are fat or skinny, I will wish to share in your happiness and troubles. Because I am your best friend.

我們都曾年輕
We Were Young Once

　　實在不敢想像，今年已將快要過去了，吾也將再增一歲了，好恐怖喲！開玩笑拉！年齡的增長，是誰也無法阻止的，最重要是活一天，感恩一天，活一天，修行一天，活一天，快樂一天。而我們也應該在有限的生命裡積極啓發智慧，讓有限的生命裡湧現韶光。若是如此，增一歲或增十歲，又有何惆悵可言。

　　男歡女愛，是要兩情相悅的，跟情投意合的。雖說這兩點缺一不可，可是專一的理念更勝一籌。而專一的愛情，在這滾滾紅塵中，又有幾人？要知道這滾滾紅塵乃業緣所成，越是執著越會被「紅塵埋沒」。這絕對沒有和專一衝突，專一也不單指在感情而已，修行更要專一，甚至做任何事都得要專一啊！

　　人生裡不是只有愛情而已，若是只有愛情的人生，那是沒有智慧及膚淺的。也是「自取滅亡」的。人生的整塊來看，妳、你必然驚覺愛情原來是那麼的一小塊。那如果妳、你夠專注，或眼尖，妳、你會發現，修行排在第一位。那是因爲夫妻本是五百年前，或多世前的冤家。就因如此，世間很少有不吵架的夫妻啊！修行排在第一位，是告訴大家，唯有修行才能夠將怨偶變成佳偶。

　　吾是修行人兼玄學家，怨偶真的看得有夠多，但願妳、

117

你有這因緣福份，觀讀到這文章，冤家宜解不宜結，祥和之氣從家庭到社會，人人幸福而美滿。新年快樂。

──── 英譯 ────────────

I can not believe that the year is over, and that I would be soon adding another year to my age. How terrifying! Ha ha, just joking! Aging is something that none of us can stop. More importantly, we must live each day in gratitude, in spiritual awareness and cultivation, and in happiness. In addition, we ought to be diligent in expanding our wisdom and consciousness in our limited life span, and to bring forth the Light in us. If we can achieve this, aging by one or ten years will not be such a depressing thought after all.

Romance between a man and a woman must be mutually pleasing and congenial. Both factors are essential, however, the notion of faithfulness is even more significant. In this current time, how many are really capable of being faithful in a relationship? You must understand that this realm we are in is entirely manifested from our karma. The more fixated we are on the notion of self, the more deeply we will be entangled in this realm. Faithfulness does not just apply to relationships alone. We need faithfulness in our spiritual cultivation and, in fact, in any thing that we do!

Life is not only about romance. If you are only concerned

with your love life, that will be ignorant and superficial. That is akin to self-destruction too. The entirety of life consists of spiritual cultivation, family ties, friendships, romance, education, contribution to society, etc. You can see that romance really only occupy a small portion of the entire spectrum, in terms of making your life a meaningful and significant one. If you are sharp and eagle-eyed, you would have noticed that I place spiritual cultivation as the first and foremost. What I am trying to tell you is that a husband and wife used to be foes with each other five hundred years ago, or many lifetimes ago. Because of this, there is rarely a couple in this world who does not fight! Only with spiritual cultivation would you be able to resolve the enmity between you and your partner, and evolve the relationship to a positive one.

I am a spiritual practitioner as well as a Metaphysicist, and have seen my fair share of couples going for each other's throats! I wish you would have the affinity and fortune to read this article and understand that it is better to resolve enmity than to make new ones. May the spirit of peace fill every family and home, and may everybody be happy and blissful. Wishing all my beloved readers a Happy New Year.

戒定慧

The Three Endeavours of Moral Discipline, Meditation and Wisdom

> 不如意十之八九，人生痛苦也很久，
> 且莫因此去喝酒，酒亂情謎禍更久。

　　戒定慧是所有修學佛法的佛弟子，都應懂應修的。它稱為三無漏學，是絕對的對的。為什麼呢？因為有漏必墮。這墮字是指六道輪迴，更慘的是三惡道求出無期。慎之，慎之。

　　在吾佛法、玄學利生的若干年裡，肯定有不少男男女女向吾吐苦水，不是口水啊！雖然有「文化」的人不多，但也不至於如此。哈！哈！哈！在他們忘我的傾訴下，也忘了吾有一定的功課與工作。吾感恩所有向吾傾訴的男女有情，因為他們的故事，多少也豐富了吾的閱歷，讓吾能夠說及寫給你們聽與看，從中警醒你們。

　　有位妙齡女郎向吾坦白，說她另有新歡。吾也直接地訓她。訓她的原固有二，「犯戒」以及根本無理由。男女拜堂成親，註冊結婚，就是婚姻上的「戒律」。維持兩人婚姻生活就是「戒律」。不能因寂寞就只聽新人笑，不知舊人哭。吾的一位弟子，也因寂寞上網和很多穿泳裝的女子玩遊戲，出國公幹也和一位女子玩曖昧。吾屢勸，他始終一意孤行。其實他早已叛離我。他本身早已被金剛神警罰，吾也告知

他，甚至特別爲他放寬戒條，救他出極苦惡道。看來吾是過於天眞。沒有實修戒、定、慧的人，又如何生起眞實感恩的心呢？天堂有路你不走，地獄無門你卻闖進去。

　　戒定慧乃佛陀聖教之正法，離苦得樂在其中，吾習之，果然眞實不虛。

Things hardly go our way in life,
The pain from life's sufferings are endless,
But do not indulge in alcohol over your sufferings,
For the consequences will prolong your woes.

The Three Endeavours of Moral Discipline, Meditation and Wisdom is a definite path which all Buddhists must understand, walk and cultivate. Why is that so? Because any of the three endeavours gone missing would result in your own fall and decline. By "fall", I meant falling into samsara, the never ending cycle of rebirth in the six realms of existence, and, more tragically, sufferings in the three lower realms with no end in sight. Beware, beware.

In my countless years of helping sentient beings through the application of Dharma and Chinese Metaphysics, there were countless men and women who "spat", not their saliva, but their bitterness at me. Ha! Ha! Ha! In the midst of pouring their woes to me, they might have forgotten that I have my own chores and work to do. Nonetheless, I am grateful for those who shared their troubles with me, for I had gained new insights and perspectives through their stories, and in turn, I am able to present them to you in my articles and advice to raise your awareness.

There was a young lady who confided in me that she had fallen for someone else. I chided her for flouting her precepts and having a wrong sense of logic. When a couple ties the knot and registers their union, they have to adhere to their marriage precepts. Maintaining their marriage life is also a precept. Loneliness is not a good reason for you to seek the company of another. I had a disciple who once, out of loneliness, befriended swimsuit-cladded ladies on Facebook games. He flirted with another lady while on working trips overseas. I advised him multiple times but my advice was not heeded. Actually, he had already left me. He was punished by the Dharma Protector and I pointed it out to him. I had even bent my rules to save him from being condemned to the evil realms. It seemed that I had been too naive. A person like him who does not cultivate the three endeavours of moral discipline, meditation and wisdom will never have the sense of gratitude. As the saying goes, "The path to Heavens beckons, yet you chose to intrude the doors of Hades."

The Three Endeavours of Moral Discipline, Meditation and

Wisdom is a sacred teaching of the Buddha, one that will free us from sufferings and achieve eternal bliss. I have walked on the path and how true it is indeed.

投奔黑暗的人
The Ones Who Deflect to Darkness

　　大多的人若談起黑暗，都會有些不大好的聯想，比如災難的到來，死亡的到來、希望破滅的到來，等等。可是，這世間也有爲數不少的「莫名奇妙」之人，總喜歡將自己讓黑暗吞噬，然後出生在極苦、極慘，既陌生又無助的境界裡，徒刑欲出無期啊！

　　有位八字被吾「驗出」有大出血的婦女，果眞在其生產第三胎的時候，大量出血，在危難中以七包血，僥倖從鬼門關回來。經過一番調養後，她再次的找吾爲她服務。吾也苦口婆心、耐心清楚地，再爲她開示，爲何她有如此之遭遇，以及未來她必被，她所謂的幸福，推向不堪設想的境地，爲她大設方便之門，好讓她在下個劫數到來之前，能夠安然度過。看來吾天眞的個性還未泯，一時忘記好了瘡疤忘了痛，以及，破的碗，就算吾再怎麼地添加法乳，這破碗始終有漏的。這樣的人其未來必定悲慘，更何況她身邊圍繞著的，大多都是前世債主！唉唷唷！實在太恐怖了。

　　一位擁有四位千金的少婦因友人介紹，到來參加「以茶會友」，之後找吾爲其批大運。吾也免費爲其四位千金測名，還有指點其目前所居之陽宅風水。原本吾並不想「拔筆相助」的，她的面相，姓名及居家風水，在在顯示其福份的次地已到了瓶頸。吾若不大力相助，後果眞不敢設想。可惜

她固執成性，好些部分並沒有速速進行。

生時已苦，死後又何苦做投奔黑暗的人呢？

When talk of darkness arises, most people would inevitably have some bad connotations, such as an impending disaster, the arrival of death and deprivation of hope, etc. However, there exist quite a number of "inexplicable" people in this world who allow themselves to be devoured by darkness. When they find themselves in utter sufferings and despair, feeling helpless and isolated, there is already no way out!

125

There was this lady whom I predicted would experience heavy bleeding from analyzing her birth chart. Indeed, whilst she was delivering her third child, she lost a huge amount of blood in the process and needed a blood transfusion of seven bags of blood, before miraculously escaping death. After recuperating for some time, she came back to seek my advice. I took great pains to patiently explain to her the Dharma so that she understood why she had to go through such adversity. I also reminded her that she would be pushed towards more unimaginable despair and sufferings, by living in this supposed happiness of hers. I opened the way for her, hoping to help her get through the next calamity safely. Alas, I am too naive for my own good, and forgot that most people will forget the pains suffered, once their wounds have healed. I should have known that no matter how much I try to fill a broken bowl with milk, it would still leak. I fear only a bleak and terrifying future awaits such people. Furthermore, she is surrounded by her karmic debtors from her past lives. How terrifying!

A young lady, with four daughters, got to know me through her friend and came to attend one of my Tea Sessions. She engaged me to analyze her luck cycles, and I gave her a free name analysis of her four daughters. In addition, I gave her some tips regarding the Feng Shui of her residence. Originally, I did not intend to help her as it was obvious from her facial features, name, as well as the Feng Shui of her house, that she was at a bottleneck due to insufficient merits in this life. If I did not lift my pen and render my help, her future would have been of dire straits. It is a pity that she is too obstinate to act quickly on my advice.

It is already a life fraught with sufferings, why plunge yourself into the sea of darkness upon death?

供奉神明的真諦
The True Significance of Deity Worship

　　還沒「正式」為師父之前，吾曾「背包游走四方」，以佛法及玄學，與廣大眾生結緣，也藉此機會，為廣大眾生排憂解難，謀取福利。當時所處理的事件，可分為幾個單元，而在這篇文章所呈獻的，是有關家中供奉神明，的眞實義及重要性。願諸位大德觀讀之後，能有正確的理念，千萬不要從俗而供奉，最後卻把神明「拋棄」、送進儲藏室……，有了惡性循環，才去東拜西拜、南求北求、到處尋訪能人異士，那眞是「運好」。若碰到「千方百計」的騙子，那可就悲哉慘哉。

　　有人將供奉已久的神明丟入垃圾槽，妻子與孩子健康、事業、婚姻等都出現問題，自己則心臟出問題。有人將供奉經年的神明「送走」，工作時從高架跌下，除了骨折、生意也沒了、兒子犯法，才去寺廟求神拜佛。有人婚姻出現問題，卻把菩薩金身關進儲藏室。這些人的愚，實在難以置信。因為這些人當中，有些是有認識師父的。就算沒有，也不可因個人的問題，任意地將佛菩薩、諸神明之金身，胡亂處理啊！一失足成千古恨，百千萬劫障礙現，又何必呢？

　　供奉神明一定要請有德有證量的師父開光。開了光的佛菩薩、諸神明金身，就是活靈活現的佛菩薩、諸神明，不但可保家也可衛國。每日虔心點香上供，唸佛持咒，頂禮禱

告，出入平安、上班或做生意皆如意、身心安泰、子女乖巧、學業進步、家和興旺是一定的。

供奉神明更是讓我們以祂們為榜樣，學習祂們的德、學習祂們的捨、學習祂們的定、學習祂們的智慧，等等等。這樣的供奉神明，最終所得一定福德圓滿。

―――― 英譯 ――――――――――――

Before I became a Master, I used to "roam the world" with my backpack. Armed with knowledge of the Dharma and Chinese Metaphysics, I would sow seeds of affinity with all whom I met, and duly help those in difficulty and seek merits on their behalf. Those multitudes of problems I have handled at that time fall under a few categories. This article aims to illustrate one particular common problem and its true significance: deity worship and enshrinement.

I hope all my virtuous readers will realise the true meaning behind this activity, and not just blindly follow the crowd. And worse still, to discard the deity statues in the end or shove them into the storeroom, never to see the light of day. This negligence will result in negative karma. This vicious cycle of negativity would send most people in a flurry seeking blessings from temples all around and from spiritual practitioners. That is "good" luck indeed! Should you bump into a fraud who swindles you of your possessions, that

would be truly disastrous.

There was this person who thrashed his deity statue and his action subsequently affected the health of his wife and children, and their respective careers and marriages. The person himself then suffered from heart problems. There was another person who sent away his deity statue after worshiping it for many years. He suffered a painful fall at work and broke his bones. His business collapsed and his son got into trouble with the law. All these drove him to seek divine help at the temples. Some people have marital problems yet they chose to keep their deity statues away in the storeroom. Their ignorance is unbelievable. Some of these people know Masters who can guide them if they ask. But even if you do not know any, please do not willfully mishandle the statues of the deities. One missed step could result in a lifetime of regrets. Is it worth it?

The consecration of the deity statues must definitely be conducted by a virtuous master, one who has achieved a certain level of attainment. The statues of the deities become energised with the presence of Buddhas, Bodhisattvas and deities after the consecration ritual, and not only do the deities protect our homes, they protect our country as well. With utmost faith and sincerity each day as we make incense offerings, chanting of mantras as well as daily prayers, our lives will be blessed in various ways like personal safety, prosperity of careers and businesses, good health, obedient children, academic progress and harmony in the family.

The worship and enshrinement of gods and deities is to enable us to learn from their exemplary attributes, to model ourselves after their highest virtues, their willingness to give, their meditative calmness, their wisdom etc. By doing so, we will surely achieve virtuous merits and bliss at the end.

命運之掌控
Take Control of Your Destiny

　　年關將至，人們也開始「整裝待發」。這整裝待發包括「做頭髮」、「修復手指腳指」，添購服裝、裝潢屋子、上網查詢流年運程、到廟裡求籤，等等。除了「應付」各種喜慶聚會，更希望來年比往年好。這些彷彿都無可厚非，但是否每個人都能稱心如意，圓滿所求？對於那些願望達成者，恭喜恭喜。對於那些無法了願者，你們除了嘆氣、碎碎唸以外，是否有靜下心來好好想，為何財神、喜神、貴神及幸運之神沒有眷顧妳、你？

　　身為修行人及玄學家的玧瑚師父，在若干年前就廢寢忘食，致力研究所這人生課題。吾的研究所得是：「做頭髮」、「修復手腳指甲」、添購服裝、裝潢屋子、到廟裡求籤、預知流年，等等，是一種補運沒錯，但距離改運，還是有一段「路程」的。那些歡歡喜喜如願的人，是他們過去世的福報，又或者在這一世，他們的有常行善布施、戒殺放生、他們有遇見善知識，對佛法信受奉行、持咒唸佛、修法拜懺，等等。而那些不行運的人，明知故犯、屢錯不改、素行不好、謗僧謗佛、罵修行人、罵神明、一毛不拔、對種種善行嗤之以鼻、師父給予的建議沒有做，等等。每年每月每日每時，都要有好的「成績單」，沒有就別想歲歲平安、「袋袋」平安，就是這麼簡單。哈！哈！哈！

其實啊！一切皆唯心。心可造天堂，心可造地獄。天地無虧欠我們，他人也無虧欠我們，由始至終都是不夠努力，沒有完成應完成的功課，才導至我們自己無法昇格。因此，根本不該怨天怨人。與其花這麼長的時間和氣力，「怨聲四起」，不如將之投於早日完成所有的功課，做個真正有福氣的人。命運之掌控要牢記，「改命必從心起，改運必先行動」。

祝　觀讀有益。

──── 英譯 ────────────────

As the end of the year edges closer, many people have started to make preparations, and that include hair styling, manicure and pedicure, new clothes, house renovation, online searches for the luck cycle predictions, temple visits for divinations, etc. Other than coping with the impending celebrations and gatherings, we surely hope that the coming year would bring forth an even better harvest. These are all inevitable, but how many of us really got our dreams fulfilled? To those who had their wishes came true, my heartiest congratulations. To those who were left disappointed, beside heaves of sighs and cursing at your bad luck, did you truly think deeply as to why the Gods of Wealth, Happiness and Fortune turned their backs on you?

As a spiritual practitioner and a Chinese Metaphysicist,

Master Dai Hu had started many years ago, sacrificing rest and meals, in my relentless pursuit of the truth to our existence. I realised that activities such as hair styling, getting a manicure and pedicure, buying new clothes, house renovation, temple visits for divinations, foretelling of luck cycle, etc, can only help to improve your lot by a bit. But they are a far way off from turning the tide to change your destiny from bad to good totally. For those who had their wishes granted, it was due to their own merits accumulated over past lifetimes. It could also be the fact that in this current lifetime, they give generously to those in need, abstain from taking lives and saves lives, learn from accomplished Dharma masters, uphold the Dharma, recite the mantras and sutras, perform repentance practice, etc. As for those whose luck is dim, they commit sins wilfully and repeatedly with no remorse, conduct themselves immorally, slander the Sangha and Buddhas, scold spiritual practitioners and the Gods, refuse to give a single cent to help those in need and yet scoff at others for doing so, did not follow the advice of Masters, etc. Every year, every month, every day, every hour of our lives, we need to produce good results, without which there is little hope of a blessed year in terms of peace, wealth and fortune. It is that simple. Ha ha ha!

As a matter of fact, all conditions are manifested from our consciousness. Your consciousness can create Heaven or it

133

can manifest Hell as your reality. Nobody owes us, not the Heavens, not the Earth, and definitely not other people. Right from the start, you have not worked hard enough. You did not complete the homework you were supposed to, and as a result, your ascension in life was halted. Thus, there is no need to point your finger at anyone. Rather than to waste your time and energy doing so, you will do well to commit them to complete your homework and be the man of your own fortune.

To have full control over your destiny, remember this faithfully:

The Change of your Destiny begins in your Heart.
The Change of your Fortune begins by taking the first step.

I wish all a bountiful harvest after reading this article

命運加倍苦的人
A Destiny with Twice The Sufferings

> 你我不說沒人知，世俗凡夫多愚癡；
> 暗室欺心消福祉，歪心速懺免時遲。

　　吾是修行人兼玄學家，啓發他人的智慧，導人向善向上，用吾的慧光照破他人的無明，明燈指引他人一條順路，是吾非常樂意、當仁不讓且常做的事。早前確實「控制不住」，如見來者身受病苦折磨、家庭不和諧、車禍中身心受創、不懷好「孕」、醫院進進出出、法庭走進走出、情海翻騰、欲海求生，等等。吾都不計時間、金錢及體力，有如「飛蛾撲火」般的給於他她們援助。有些客人所面對的重重困難，眞實迎刃而解。有些客人之問題則未見明顯改善，甚至所面對的障礙叫吾不盡開始懷疑自己的能力。

　　在懷疑自己及不解的時光中，吾仍然積極、精進地研究與「明查暗訪」，希望不久且很快的，提昇吾之技能，繼續圓滿吾之發願。

　　那些無法改善自身問題的人，在吾「明查暗訪」後的結論是：無神論、強自己主張及意見、明知故犯、無慚愧心無懺悔心、素行不佳、好奇而已、從俗而已……等等。

　　若不幸妳、你是其中的一種，玳瑚師父在此誠心勸妳、你，不要浪費時間和錢來找吾。因爲，祇要是上方所述之

類，必定沒有福份扭轉乾坤、反敗爲勝的。佛眼如電眼，我們所做的一切，佛知之甚詳。更何況，鬼神是佈滿十方法界的。我們根本沒有「隱私」。我們的起心動念，鬼神早已知之，因此，奉勸各位若想要改善命運及自身問題，快快打掃自己的心房，不要再「胡思亂想」，這樣來找玳瑚師父，才能相得益彰。

———— **英譯** ————

No one will know if you and I kept mum,
The worldly man is full of ignorance,
They deceived themselves in the dark and have their merits shaved,
Repent hastily before it is too late.

I am a spiritual practitioner as well as a Chinese Metaphysicist, one who inspires wisdom and kindness in others, and uses my light of wisdom to dispel the ignorance of others and lead them onto a smooth path. This is something that I do most willingly, without the slightest hesitation. In my early days, I could not control myself whenever I met sentient beings suffering from sickness, family disharmony, bodily injuries due to accidents, fertility problems, difficult pregnancies, endless hospital visits, legal woes, troubled relationships etc. I would spare no effort in terms of time, money and strength, almost like a moth

attracted to the fire, to render aid to the troubled persons. I managed to resolve the problems of some clients. But there were others whose sufferings showed no signs of abating, and this led me to doubt my own abilities.

During those times of self doubt and lack of clarity, I still persisted in my research and investigation in hope that in the days to come or perhaps very soon, my abilites will raise to a greater height and I will continue towards the fulfillment of my vows.

According to my research and investigation, those people who are unable to turn their fortunes around fall into the following categories:

They are atheists;
They are very self-opinionated;
They transgress willfully;
They are non-repentant;
They have bad moral conduct;
They are merely curious;
They conform to traditions & conventions;
etc.

Should you unfortunately fall into the above categories, Master Dai Hu sincerely advises that you do not waste your money and time to engage my service. Because you will not have sufficient merits to turn the tide and change your fortune for the better. The Eyes of the Buddha are omnipresent, from which our words and actions cannot escape. Furthermore, the gods and the deva gods are everywhere, and we have absolutely no privacy. Our every thought and intention are already known to them. Thus, I will advise those who wish to better their fortune and solve their problems to sweep your heart clean. Do not engage in flights of fancy. This way, you will stand to benefit from engaging my service.

和陽光約會吧！
Let's Have A Date With The Sunshine!

在〈向日〉的文章中，吾有寫到自己很喜愛陽光。陽光真實給人希望，欣欣向榮及朝氣的覺受。看看那些戶外的運動健兒們，曬得一身銅色膚色，給人一種非常健康的感覺，同時也給人很陽剛的印象。古時候的人們，日出而做，日落而息，他們都很健康，少病痛且長壽。相反那些不曬太陽，又或者少曬太陽的人，似乎身體較差些。

夏季雖然會很炎熱，但這季節是四季中，最能讓人感覺到欣欣向榮的一個季節。萬物在春天開始綻放，在夏天是最強盛時期。就如春天百花開，夏天百花爭妍。美國加利福尼亞州的橙為何世界有名？因為那裡的陽光充足呀！南非的水菓也很佳，這都是因為陽光充足的關係啊！

玄學中批八字的部份，也需要掌握好四季的強弱時期，才能夠更準確的，找出當事人的八字，身強或身弱，還有其八字的的其餘用神。夏天當然屬火，其特性肯定是陽剛味足，且積極有進取心。一天二十四小時中的午時，也就是上午十一時至午後一時，也是人體體內，血液活動力最強的時段，人的精神與體力，在這時段也是最強的。因此，可別把這大好的時段，跑去睡覺哦！那是非常浪費的。

天下萬物包括人類，都是需要陽光的。沒有陽光就是黑暗。黑暗所滋生的問題是不堪設想的。這席話相信唯有雙目

失明的朋友，最能明白。陽光給於我們保護、陽光給於我們健康的膚色，陽光給於我們亮麗的外型，等等。啊……如此的這般的美好，快和陽光約會吧！

英譯

In my previous article titled "Looking Towards The Sun", I wrote about my love for the sun. The sun radiates hope, prosperity and energy for many people. Look at those outdoor athletes and their beautiful tan. It totally exudes an image of good health and positivity. People from ancient times lived their lives according to the daily cycle of the Sun. They rose in the morning to work, and retired for rest, once the Sun set in the evening. They were healthy, enjoyed a long life and were generally free from sickness. On the other hand, those of you today who do not get much of the sun seem to have poorer health disposition.

The summer heat may be blistering but this is the only season in a year that makes one feel prosperous. All things bloom in Spring and are at their best in Summer. Like the flowers that awaken in Spring but bloom at its brightest in Summer, fighting to be the best among the rest. Oranges from California are renowned because of the ample sunlight they received. Fruits from South Africa are fantastic also due to the same reason!

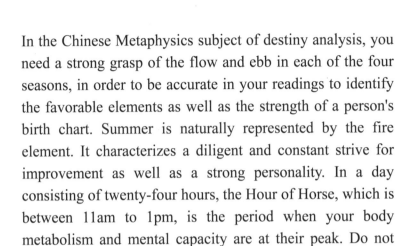

In the Chinese Metaphysics subject of destiny analysis, you need a strong grasp of the flow and ebb in each of the four seasons, in order to be accurate in your readings to identify the favorable elements as well as the strength of a person's birth chart. Summer is naturally represented by the fire element. It characterizes a diligent and constant strive for improvement as well as a strong personality. In a day consisting of twenty-four hours, the Hour of Horse, which is between 11am to 1pm, is the period when your body metabolism and mental capacity are at their peak. Do not waste this time by running off to bed!

All living things in this world, including human beings, need sunlight. In the absence of light comes darkness. Negative issues that arise from darkness are unthinkable. Our friends who are blind can surely testify to that. Sunlight gives us protection and a healthy glowing skin and outlook etc. Ah, it is such a blessing. Let's quickly fix a date with the sunshine!

學佛之正
Learn the Righteous Way of the Buddha

妳、你每天看著家裡供奉的佛像，有沒有學祂的正？

祂坐的正，坐的自在，坐的莊嚴。

人坐姿正，行為正，心就正。

彌勒佛的笑，在笑天下眾生的愚癡。

彌勒佛的肚大，因為能容納天下人不能夠容納的事情。

人正，氣則陽。人邪，氣則陰。

陰者下地獄，陽者昇天。

陰氣入侵，健康事業皆不順。陽氣旺者，妻財子祿皆旺。

衰旺，請君自行選擇。

───── 英譯 ─────

You look at the statue of the Buddha in your house everyday, so do you ever learn from His righteous ways?

The righteous posture in which the Buddha sits mirrors His inner calm and dignity.

When the sitting posture of a man is proper and his actions are righteous, his heart will follow.

Maitreya Buddha, or "Laughing Buddha", wears a laugh on His face because He is laughing at the ignorance of all sentient beings.

He has a big belly, because He can tolerate what mankind is unable to.

When a man is righteous, his life energy is yang (positive). When a man is evil, his life energy is yin (negative).

A person with yin energy will be banished to the depths of Hades, while a person with yang energy shall ascend to the Heavens.

When the yin energy intrudes, your health, career and other aspects of your life will flounder and deteriorate. Likewise, when the yang energy is prevalent, your life will flourish and prosper.

To take the path of prosperity or decline? It is entirely your own choice.

宗教的真實義
The True Essence of Religion

　　妳、你現在是否正處在，選擇妳、你「心靈方向」的十字路口，眼前也似乎充滿迷霧般的茫茫然，而「無所適從」呢？若是的話，這篇文章就是玳瑚師父為你們，向虛空中的高靈們祈禱，將這篇非常重要的文章，傳送到你們休閒觀讀的空間裡。讓你們在「明燈的指引」下，清清楚楚、明明白白地選擇你們最終的「心靈方向」。

　　很多人被很多人指責迷信，事實上是有跡可尋的。因為那些被指責為迷信的人們，言談舉止根本跟宗教，所要傳達的理念，完全是背道而馳。他們向所信仰的祈求，馬票贏多多、炒樓買股票致富、娶得美人歸，等等。天啊！曾幾何時，宗教變成增長個人貪念、欲望的媒體？如果宗教是這般的迷惑人心，它如何讓世人尊敬之、依靠之、學習之呢？因此，很明顯的，這些人兒們錯解了宗教的真實義。

　　全世界的宗教，相信都有幾個共同點。

一、導人向善向上。
二、勸人珍惜生命、尊重生命。
三、感恩於一切。
四、伸出援手於一切有情。（不是多啦A夢。）
五、不可有分別心，等等。

　　宗教所傳達的，永遠是和平與和諧。絕對沒有所謂被批評就教人帶著炸藥、炸彈，向批評者報復。這樣的一種行事，世界如何及幾時才能真正的和平與和諧呢？這些簡直是變相極端啊！

　　佛教教主南無本師釋迦牟尼佛，教導吾等說，修行有如調琴，不能太緊亦不能太鬆，因為琴弦太緊會斷。琴弦太鬆則無法彈出美妙的音樂。這就是有名的中庸之道。這也是宗教的真實義。依著這正確理念，才能算選對真正能引領妳、你，心靈昇華的信仰。

────── 英譯 ──────────────────

Are you presently at a crossroad when it comes to choosing your spiritual direction, with no clear sight ahead and no obvious choice? If you are, then this article written by Master Dai Hu is just the one for you. I prayed to the higher beings in the Infinite Void that this important article will be delivered to you during your leisure reading time. May this article shine a light of wisdom onto you and, in total clarity and understanding, lead you towards your eventual spiritual direction.

Many people would accuse many others of being superstitious, and this could be explained. Many of those being accused of superstitious exhibit behaviour and thinking that is incongruent to what the religion prescribes to. These superstitious folks pray to strike the lottery, to become rich through stock or property investment, to marry a beautiful wife, etc. Oh dear, since when did religion become a tool for us to indulge ourselves in our ever increasing greed and desires? If a religion throws dust in its believers' eyes, how will it command the respect of the people, and be depended on as well as to learn from? Thus it is obvious that these superstitious folks have misunderstood the true essence of religion.

All the religions in this world have a few commonalities. Firstly, they guide their believers towards a virtuous life. Secondly, they teach us to treasure and respect life. Thirdly, they advocate a sense of gratitude for everything in life. Fourthly, they encourage us to always lend a helping hand to those in need. Last but not least, they teach us to view all as equal. Religion is always preaching peace and harmony. A true religion will never ask its believers to harm those who criticise the religion. Such violence will never bring about real peace and harmony in this world. Such violence is practically extremism!

The Shakyamuni Buddha taught us that spiritual cultivation is like playing a lute. The string of the lute can neither be too tight nor too loose. The string will break if it is too tight.

On the other hand, the lute will not produce melodious notes if the string is too loose. This is the well-known Middle Path, and it also reflects the true essence of religion. With this guiding principle, may you choose the right religion to advance yourself spiritually.

明因果無煩惱
Understand the Law of Karma for a Worry-free Life

　　吾站在魚缸前唸往生短咒的習慣，已經很多很多年了。
（至少十二年以上。）

　　吾唸的往生短咒，無數無數遍。

　　往生短咒：

　　往生淨土，超生出苦，

　　南無阿彌陀佛，

　　南無阿彌陀佛，

　　南無阿彌陀佛。

　　受益的畜類，算也算不清了。

　　吾在餐館裡唸，在有飼養魚的客人家裡唸，在池塘旁
唸，在超市的肉類區唸，路過「橫死街頭」的蝸牛昆蟲時
唸，坐車經過墳墓區（臺灣和馬來西亞較多）唸，讀到報紙
的死亡事件也為亡者唸。

　　每一次唸，至少七遍。

　　每一次唸，都很用心。

　　每一次唸，也提醒它們不要埋怨自己的遭遇，因為前世
的錯，今世還。要趕緊懺悔，才能離苦得樂。

　　但，終究只是吾一個人的力量。

　　所以，這往生短咒，吾教了很多弟子、學生和客人。至
今，不知有多少人還能保持這發心。

　　吾看魚缸裡的水族，不但越來越多，連一些稀有的品種也有。感慨人類的貪念越來越重。

　　吾看到水族們的恐懼、絕望、無助、嘴巴的傷痕，還有眼裡的恨和無明。吃下去，就是把它們的瞋和痴的能量轉移到我們的身上，我們的身心會好嗎？爲什麼人類患癌的病例越來越多？妳、你以爲這些癌的腫瘤是從哪裡來？

　　眞的有必要爲了貪「新鮮」而吃活海鮮嗎？

　　舉凡飲食業，都必定有殺生。而所謂殺生，不單是指拿刀殺生害命，凡一切惡毒詛咒他人、獻計害人等等，皆屬殺生。

　　今世妳、你殺它，來世它殺妳、你。這就是因果分毫不欠妳、你。一命還一命，謂之公平。未來家中也會出現病弱、難帶、忤逆、痼疾，等等，之不祥子女。愼之，愼之。

　　願大家明因果，無煩無惱過日子。

　　　　人生切莫把心欺，神鬼昭彰放過誰，
　　　　善惡到頭終有報，只爭來早與來遲。

　（在外，少刷手機，多唸一遍往生短咒吧！）

—— 英譯 ——

I have been habitually reciting the short Mantra for Rebirth in Pure Land in front of numerous fish tanks, for many

many years. (At least ten years.)

I have recited this mantra countless times.

Short Mantra for Rebirth in Pureland:

wǎng	shēng	jìng	tǔ		
往	生	淨	土		
chāo	shēng	chū	Kǔ		
超	生	出	苦		
nán	mó	ā	mí	tuó	fó
南	無	阿	彌	陀	佛
nán	mó	ā	mí	tuó	fó
南	無	阿	彌	陀	佛
nán	mó	ā	mí	tuó	fó
南	無	阿	彌	陀	佛

And I have lost count of how many animals I have helped.

I recite the mantra in the restaurants, at clients' homes with aquariums, beside the ponds, at the meat section of supermarkets, when I spot the carcasses of insects and snails on the streets, when I pass by cemeteries (mostly in Taiwan and Malaysia) and when I read of death cases in the newspapers.

Every time I recite the mantra, it will be at least seven times.

Every time I recite the mantra, I do so with my heart in it.

Every time after I do so, I will remind the animals not to bear grudges for their sad ending, for what we did wrong in our past lives, we pay it back this life. They must repent soon to get out of their sufferings and attain eternal bliss.

Alas, it is still my effort alone.

I have imparted this mantra to many disciples, students and clients. Till date, how many of them still bother to do so as I have taught?

The greed of mankind shows no sign of abating. Not only is the quantity of fishes in the aquariums increasing but there are more and more rare species among them. Beyond the wounds on their lips, I saw in them the fear, hopelessness, helplessness and most obviously, the hatred and ignorance in their eyes. If we consume them, we are taking in their energies of hatred and ignorance into our bodies. What will happen then to our physical and mental states? Why are cancer cases on the rise? Where did you think the cancer tumours come from?

Is it that necessary to consume live seafood for the sake of "freshness"?

In the food and beverage industry, there is definitely killing. However, it is not only with knives and choppers that we commit the act of killing. Cursing others, devising ways to harm others etc, is akin to killing.

In this life, you take the lives of other sentient beings. In the next lifetime, they will come after yours. This is the Law of Karma, which ensures real equality. An eye for an eye, in all fairness. In the future, you will see your offspring being prone to sickness, disobedience and rebellion. Please act carefully.

I wish for everyone to understand the truth of the Law of Karma in order to lead a life of no worry.

As we live, do not deceive your own heart,
For the Gods and Spirits are everywhere and no one will be spared,
The Good and the Bad will get what they deserve,
It is just but a matter of time.

(Spend less time on your mobile phone and instead, more time to recite the Short Mantra for Rebirth to Pureland!)

武動生命
"Martial" Up Your Life!

　　曾經多次爲殘障人士落淚。心想若有一天，自己也成殘障人士，那該怎麼辦？人生未完成的事情，又該如何是好？學佛開啓了智慧，這種種的「無知」，早已轉化成正知正見的光環，保護著吾免受「顛倒妄想」之苦。認清了身體殘障實不可怕，最怕是「心靈」或「思想」殘障。可偏偏到處皆有這類人。阿彌陀佛。

　　在現實生活中，吾就常常與「心靈」或「思想」殘障之人接觸。若這類人祇出現於客人群中，相信是比較好些的。怕就怕，這類人也出現於徒弟和學生中，那就是一種「造化」了。前世債，今世還，是一種因果，也是一種公平定律啊！「智慧光環」下，唯有「兵來將擋，水來土掩」了。

　　吾曾「施法」幫助差一點進入「殘障」範圍的人。吾也曾因過度運動，傷了筋脈，整整一個多月「徘徊」於殘障邊緣，眞是險過剃頭。還好有佛菩薩的靈光加持，以及醫師的基因傳承，讓吾得以通過自己獨創的「體功」，醫好因過度運動的傷痛。有了實在的經歷與心得，吾更有信心將吾所創之「體功」，廣傳於有此需要及有緣想學以保健之人。

　　先前有提到，吾常常接觸「心靈」或「思想」殘障之人。那一天吾在授課之餘，突然心血來潮，現場示範一些招數，頓時讓吾之徒弟及學生興高采烈，要求吾「上演」多一

153

點片段，吾也就在一夜間，成爲「萬千寵愛於一身」的「功夫巨星」。樂此不疲的代價，是一個字——累。哈！哈！哈

有句話說得對，「預防勝於治療」。相信每個人，都有可能殘障。

更相信每個人都不願意殘障。既然如此，大家應趁能動的時候，多動及勤於動。人說：生命在於運動。吾則說：一起來「武動生命」吧！異曲而同功。哈！哈！哈！

英譯

My tears fell on several occasions in the past when I saw disabled persons. I ponder if one day I become disabled, what will I do? What will happen to those unfinished tasks and aspirations? With new insights and wisdom from learning the Dharma, these ignorant thoughts have long been transformed under the guiding light of Right Knowledge and Right View, thus protecting me from being tortured by unwholesome thoughts. I recognized that physical disability is not fearful. The most fearful disability is those that cripple your mind and soul. But alas, there are people suffering from such crippling disabilities everywhere. Amithaba.

In real life, I am often in contact with people of mind & soul disabilities. If these people are from my clientele, I guess it is not that bad. What will be scary is if they are among my

disciples and students. That would be my fate then. Debts from previous lives have to be cleared in this lifetime. This is karma and the way the Universe enforces fairness and equality. With the light of wisdom, I can only counter measure with measure, come what may.

I once helped a person who was close to being disabled. On another occasion, I injured myself due to over-exercise. For more than a month, I was bordering on the edge of physical disability. It was a really close shave. I am fortunate to receive the blessings of the Buddhas and Bodhisattvas, and coupled with the medical knowledge I inherited from my late father, I was able to heal myself with my self-invented techniques. Tested over time and with extensive practice, I am now more confident to impart these techniques to those who need help or wish to learn it for their fitness regimens.

Previously, I mentioned that I am often in contact with people of mind and soul disabilities. That day whilst I was giving lessons, I had this sudden impulse and demonstrated some moves. That got my students excited momentarily and requesting for more. Overnight, I became a "Kung Fu superstar" adulated by the millions. The price to pay for such happiness? Utter tiredness. Ha ha ha!

The phrase "Prevention is better than cure." is right. I believe everyone of us is possibly disabled, and I also believe none of us wants to be that way. Thus, let us all exercise more diligently while we still can! It is said that physical exercise is the essence to life. Well, for me, I say let's kick some martial buzz into our lives! All roads lead to Rome, don't they? Ha ha ha!

持咒唸佛
Recitation Of The Buddha's Name & Mantra

　　大概兩個星期前的一個週日晚上，面見一位男客人，給他新的名字。他看到吾在進食前會持往生咒，後來，好奇地問吾：「師父，晚上持咒不會招很多鬼來嗎？」

　　唸「南無阿彌陀佛」、「南無觀世音菩薩」等為唸佛，而唸「嗡阿彌爹哇些」、「嗡嘛呢唄咪吽」等就是在持咒。那咒跟佛號，可以任選一嗎？最好兩個一起唸，因為唸佛是呼喚佛，而持咒是直接觸碰佛的心。祂知道妳、你有難，馬上會派護法來幫助妳、你。一個是衣領，一個是衣服，衣服不可以沒有領，沒有領就不成衣服，所以唸佛和持咒最好能合起來，才會功德圓滿。

157

　　用數珠來持咒唸佛，每拔一顆珠，就是把一個佛的種子深深地植入我們的心裡面，那我們未來必定能夠成佛。用兩手握住數珠，是代表兩手都在轉法輪，而將數珠握在妳、你的胸膛前，更是提醒妳、你要一心唸佛。持咒唸佛時，不可以想其他東西，妳、你的咒音要出口、入耳、印心，就會產生一種力量出來。

　　持咒唸佛時，會有一種結界，設了一道防線，所以這些「第三者」根本不能夠進來。因此，不用害怕晚上持咒唸佛會引「第三者」出現，這是人一種錯誤的想法，心的作用。妳、你在持咒的時候，佛菩薩都在放光照妳、你。周圍都有

佛光注照時，這些「好兄弟」很難近妳、你身。

第二，妳、你唸了，她、他聽了，她、他也能夠得度。我們人都有業障，也一定會有纏身靈。我們持咒時，我們的纏身靈也會聽到，她、他也跟著唸的時候，將來我們全部都能一起成佛，這就是大慈大悲。

持咒唸佛不一樣，但兩個最好合在一起，會有很大的力量，能夠推毀一切挫障，給妳、你人生走得比較順。有人設起障礙給妳、你，要給妳、你倒，陷害妳、你，當妳、你唸比較多的時候，那些障礙會倒，妳、你就能夠通行無阻。

―――― 英譯 ――――

On one weekday night, two weeks ago, I met a male client to give him his newly-minted Chinese name. He saw me chanting the Rebirth in Pureland mantra before I consumed my food. Out of curiosity, he asked me, "Master, doesn't chanting during the night attract many spirits to come?"

Reciting "Namo Amituofo", "Namo Guan Shi Yin Pu Sa", etc is called recital of Buddha's name, whereas when you chant "Om Amideva Hrih", "Om Mani Pae Me Hom", you are chanting a mantra. Between reciting the Buddha's name and a mantra, do you choose only one? It would be ideal to both recite the Buddha's name and chant the mantra as the former is akin to calling out to a particular Buddha or

Bodhisattva, while the latter is akin to touching Their hearts. The Buddha or Bodhisattva would know once you are in need, and would send the Dharma Protectors to your aid. Just like a shirt would not be complete without a collar, your merits would be complete if you recite the Buddha's name and chant His Mantra at the same time.

When you use mala beads to recite the Buddha's name or chant his Mantra, for every bead that you count, you are planting a Buddha seed deep into your subconsciousness, and these seeds would ripen in the future for you to attain Buddhahood. To hold your mala beads with both hands symbolises you turning the wheel of Dharma with both your hands. And to hold your mala beads in front of your chest is a reminder for you to be focused when chanting.

159

You should not have other thoughts when you are chanting. The sounds of your recitation should go in your ears and leave an imprint in your heart, and from there, a kind of power will emerge. Recitation of the Buddha's name and mantra is a form of demarcation and sets a boundary, making it impossible for the "third parties" to come in. Hence, there is no reason to think that chanting at night will attract the "invisibles". This is a misconception. When you are chanting, the Buddhas and Bodhisattvas will shine Their light on you. When you are surrounded by Their Light, the "invisibles" will not be able to get near you.

Secondly, when you are chanting or reciting, it would be audible to the other people in your surroundings, and these people would inevitably plant the seeds of salvation for themselves as well. We come with our own karmic debts and debtors. As you chant the mantra, your karmic debtors will hear and might even follow in your footsteps and start chanting for their own salvation too. We could all attain Buddhahood together. This is great compassion.

Chanting the mantra is different from reciting the Buddha's name. However, by combining both of them would generate great power to help you overcome the obstacles in life, allowing you a smoother journey ahead. People might set up hurdles to make you fall or harm you. When the frequency of your chanting increases, these obstacles will be removed and you shall pass through them effortlessly.

迎接善光的那一天起
From the Day I Received the Light of Virtue

　　二十五年前有位小居士幾乎每次見到吾，就歡歡喜喜地與吾分享佛法。當年他雖是居士，可在吾的眼裡，他有如小沙彌的化身，善良且不記吾之失禮，樂意渡化吾這「邊緣少年」。哈……！我們已失去聯絡多年，誠心祝福他，依然沐浴佛光裡，善業早圓滿，證得明心見性。

　　以上是玟瑚師父，一小段最初接觸佛法的敘述。吾真正開始研習佛法，也就是皈依，則是在農曆的八月十五，有道是，月到中秋分外明，吃餅賞月千情趣。更有，每逢佳節倍思親。吾這思親指的，是你我他共同的本源。若然知曉吾之意，方為同道中人啊！原本吾皈依並不是這「月圓之日」。之前欲皈依，兩次皆失敗。第三次才成功，而那一天正逢中秋佳節，這當中似乎有些寓意，這寓意著吾上求佛果、下化眾生、利己利他、冥陽兩利，將會是圓滿的。

　　在還沒學佛前，總以為自己在家中、在學校、在工作崗位上，都是善的。一直到了皈依學佛，才如夢初醒般地覺察到，原來吾所認為的善，並不是真善。因為真善是不計較、無所謂、守戒、懺悔、施恩莫忘報、勤修戒定慧、熄滅貪瞋癡、一切皆感恩的。這些智慧乃是吾迎接善光的那一天起，實修真實佛法所證得。或許妳、你會有所問，人生在世開心快樂不就好嗎？開心快樂無可厚非，但沒有修行的開心快

161

樂，往往都會滋生很多過失出來，最終依然在輪迴痛苦中「欲走還留」，這就不是智慧，而是愚癡啊！

玳瑚師父由衷地期盼著，妳、你也會有妳、你迎接善光的那一天，證入永恆的快樂光明裡，向所有的痛苦說「拜拜」。感恩。

—— 英譯 ——

Twenty five years ago, there was a young Buddhist lay practitioner who would happily share the Dharma with me almost every time he saw me. Although he was a lay practitioner, in my eyes, he was like a little novice monk. He was kind and did not mind my insolence, and willingly shared the Dharma to deliver the wayward youth in me. Ha! We have since lost touch with each other for many years, and I sincerely send him my best wishes that he is still basking in the light of the Buddha, that all his virtuous deeds will come to fruition, and that he will attain total clarity of his mind and revelation of Buddha nature.

The above paragraph illustrated, in a small part, my initial contact with the Dharma. I started my formal practice of the Dharma, and that would mean taking refuge, on the 15th Day of the 8th Lunar Month (Mid-Autumn Festival). As the saying goes, "The moon on Mid-Autumn is especially clear and pristine, eating moon cakes and appreciating the full

moon bring wondrous delights in life." Another one goes, "The longing of our kins exacerbates during the festive season". The kinship that I mentioned refer to the common Origin of you and me. For those of you who understand my meaning, we indeed walk the same path! I did not originally intend to take refuge in the Triple Gems on this day of the Full Moon. The past two tries ended up in failure. Only upon the third attempt was I successful, and that day coincided with the Mid-Autumn Festival. This seems to signify that my pursuits of Enlightenment, deliverance of the sentient beings, benefiting both self and others, both the living and the dead, shall come to perfect fruition.

Before I learnt the Dharma, I always thought that what I did at home, in school or in my job were of virtuous in nature. Only after I have taken refuge and started learning the Dharma did the awakening occurred. I realised that my previous notions of kindness and virtues were not authentic. Being truly virtuous or kind means not being calculative nor expectant. It involves upholding of precepts and the act of repentance. It teaches us to remember and to repay kindness bestowed upon us. It promotes diligence in cultivating the Three Endeavours (Discipline, Meditation, Wisdom) and douses the fire of Greed, Hatred and Ignorance. It advocates gratitude towards all we have in life. This wisdom was bestowed upon me from the day I received the virtuous light and actualized my Dharma practice and spiritual cultivation diligently. Some of you may ask, "Is it not enough to just be happy during our lifetime?". It is inevitable for one to crave for happiness, but without spiritual cultivation, our quest for happiness will breed more misdeeds that will eventually lead us down the path of endless sufferings in Samsara. This is not wisdom, but ignorance.

Master Dai Hu sincerely looks forward to the day when you receive the light of virtue into your life, enter into an eternal state of light and bliss, and bid farewell to all sufferings.

My gratitude to all.

是時候修福修德了
Now is the Time to Cultivate your Merits and Morals

　　近期無論是勘察地理、批大運、批流年、撰名或開光等等，竟然碰不到一位眞有福德者。妳、你祇要找得到吾，吾必定非常「使勁」的，爲妳、你謀取福利。可是，妳、你可曾想過，若是有一天吾「成道」了，吾隱居了，吾退休了，我們失去了聯絡，或有人「拆散」我們……，那時侯誰來代妳、你的業，誰能及願意爲妳、你「使勁」地謀取福利，這些問題眞的應該靜下心來認眞想一想。

　　妳、你又可曾思維，爲何富不過三代，爲何沒人欣賞妳、你，沒人擁戴妳、你，妳、你和友人同時進入公司，妳、你倆有同等的文憑，薪水及受重視的程度，卻不太一樣、好不容易創業，不到一二年，就結束營業。還有更多更多的人與事，一幕一幕的上演著，這到底是爲甚麼，爲甚麼，爲甚麼……？

　　在妳、你聲聲問爲甚麼的當兒，妳、你其實也應該兼問，妳、你何德何能，擁有這一切的福報？我們都應該善用我們與身俱來的「慧根」（腦也），思維再思維爲何天常復、地常載、樹會結果、山谷會有清泉、百草中有藥能治病，等等等。這些都是大自然的教育，教導我們貢獻是一切，欣欣向榮的來源。相反的，自私又自利的人，她、他永遠也不會有「豐收」的一天，原因實在是簡單不過，因爲她、他「產量」不多啊！別再「碎碎唸」、別再執著了，要

165

「豐收」要「美好」，是時候該修福修德了。

On my recent work assignments, be it Feng Shui audits, luck cycle analysis, name analysis or consecretion etc, I was surprised that I could not meet a single client who truly had merits and morals. As long as you can find me, I will strive my best to bring benefits to you. However, have you ever thought of this: what if one day I attain enlightenment, or I go into reclusion, or I retire, or we lose contact or got separated by others? When this day arrives, who will be there to bear the brunt of your negative karma? Who will be there to do his best and bring benefits to you? This is a question which you need to quieten your mind and give it a serious thought.

Have you ever pondered why our wealth will not last beyond our third generation? Why do others not appreciate and treat you well? Why do they not support you? You and your friend started a new job at the same time in the same company, with similar qualifications. However your salary paled in comparison to him or her, and you were not as highly valued either. You struggled and finally started your own business, but it folded within a year or two. More and more of such scenarios continue to happen in your life. Why

are these happening? Why? Why?

As this question keeps swirling in your head, you should, at the same time, ask yourself, "What merits or morals do I have to deserve the good fortune?" We should make good use of our inherent wisdom (the brain) to think and ponder. Why is the Heaven benevolent? Why is the Earth all encompassing? Why does the tree bear fruits? Why is there spring water among the valleys? Why are there herbs among the plants that can cure diseases? etc. These are lessons taught to us by Mother Nature. She teaches us that selfless giving is the source of our own prosperity. On the contrary, people who are selfish and self-centred will never experience bountiful harvest in their lives. The reason is simply that these people did not sow enough seeds for that to happen! Quit the incessant whining and self attachment. If you desire a good harvest and all things great, the time is now to cultivate your merits and morals.

167

洗滌業障
Washing Away Negative Karma

　　每次去臺灣參加法會後，儘管睡眠不足，第一個覺受就是一種眞的徹底的淨化。吾眞的很感恩有這麼殊勝的法緣。

　　我們只要離開了修行這兩個字，我們每分每秒都是在增加我們身內身外的塵埃。這塵埃不去除，將來就變成一種障礙，叫做業障。那個時候，就不要怨天尤人。

　　妳、你要好，我也要好。大家都想要好。那妳、你有去思考，如何去爭取妳、你要的好嗎？是每天在公司搞政治，打小報告，妒忌這個，嫌東嫌西，講是非恨人這些嗎？那我可以告訴妳、你，妳、你怎麼找最厲害的算命師，妳、你的命依然是不可能改好的。

―― 英譯 ――

Every time after I participated in a puja ceremony in Taiwan, despite the lack of sleep, the very first feeling I experienced was thorough purification. I am deeply grateful for this rare Dharmic affinity.

The moment we stray away from our spiritual cultivation, we will start accumulating the worldly filth of defilement both inside and outside our body, by the second and minute.

As long as we do not get rid of this filth, it will eventually manifest into obstacles, a sign of negative karma. Once that happens, please blame no one but yourself.

You wish for a better life and so do I. Everyone wants to do well in life. But have you ever given it any thought on how to achieve the prosperity you want? Are you going to get it by meddling in office politics, back-stabbing others, hating and being jealous of others, finding fault with others and engage in bad-mouthing? If that is so, let me tell you this: even if you engage the best fortune teller, you will never be able to turn your life around.

風調雨順，國泰民安
The Way To a Prosperous & Peaceful Nation with Favourable Weather

　　「風調雨順，國泰民安」這八個字，相信對一般人而言，絕對不會太陌生。聽是聽過，但妳、你是否真實明白，這八個字箇中的道理及含義？又或者，妳、你可會認真思維，其中含義及道理呢？要知道，真正的能人，真正的學者，她、他必會或必定付出時間付出精力，做了一番研究與考驗後，得到了答案和結論，才對有關事項，給於定論。這樣才是名符其實的，能人及學者。

　　「國泰民安」，是指國家富強、安定繁榮，百姓人民豐衣足食、都有就業機會。這樣看似乎沒什麼不妥，可是又為何有前面那一句「風調雨順」呢？原來這說明了，人世間的一切，真的和宇宙大自然有關。不是嗎？大家靜下心來想想看，有四季的國家，與沒有四季的國家的分別。天災地禍多的國家，與天災地禍少的國家的分別。想啊想，妳、你就會明白「風調雨順」是多麼的重要啊！

　　其實「風調雨順」不是一般人所知道的「風調」、「雨順」。只有真正知其深意，並實在且非常努力的去修持，每一個國家，甚至全世界，才會有「風調雨順，國泰民安」的那麼一天的到來。要不然，這八個字衹是「天方夜譚」，不如將之拋出腦後。

　　風，即是體內的氣，外在的呼吸。雨即是體內的水份及養份。而水份及養份，都得靠氣來傳送及導引，到最後「氣定神閒」，自然能夠包容一切，國家及全世界，也就真的風調雨順，國泰民安了。

英譯

The Chinese phrase "風調雨順，國泰民安", literally translated as "Smooth Winds and Favourable Rains, Prosperous Nation and Peaceful Society" should be quite familiar to most people. You might have heard of this phrase many times but do you really understand the essence of it? Or have you ever pondered deeply about the deeper meaning of this phrase? You must know that a person with real ability and wisdom surely would have committed time and effort to investigate all possibilities before coming to a final conclusion. This is the true billing of a able and learned person.

"Prosperous Nation and Peaceful Society" refers to a strong and wealthy nation, peaceful and prosperous with her people well-clothed, well-fed and gainfully employed. There seems to be nothing wrong with the above, but why do we precede the phrase with this "Smooth Winds and

Favourable Rains"? This goes to show that this material world is heavily linked to the Universe and natural phenomenons. Is it not so? Let us all be still and ponder over it. What is the difference between a country with four seasons and a country with no seasonal change? What is the difference between a country stricken with natural and man-made disasters and one who experiences very little or none at all. After much thinking, you would have realised that having "Smooth Winds and Favourable Rains" is so important!

In actual fact, the phrase "Smooth Winds and Favourable Rains" cannot be taken literally as really having smooth and favourable weather. The real essence lies in the true and diligent cultivation of every person, nation and even the whole world to truly realise the the day when the whole world will have "Smooth Winds and Favourable Rains". If we miss the point, it is nothing but just a far-fetched fairy tale, best to be shelved at the back of your head.

The wind is represented by the Qi (life energy) inside your body, reflected in your breath. The rain is represented by the water and nutrients in your body. These water and nutrients rely heavily on the Qi in the body to move and guide their passage in your body, reaching a state of stillness and

oneness of the mind. In this state, you will naturally be able to tolerate and embrace everything, a country and the world. That would be totally aligned with the phrase "Smooth Winds and Favourable Rains, Prosperous Nation and Peaceful Society".

修行在個人
Spiritual Cultivation Is Your Own Responsibility

　　若干年前，有客人對吾說，他們想買靠近吾住的地方，甚至最靠近吾住的單位，害吾在那段日子，彷若電影中的「忍者」，什麼意思？「神出鬼沒」。他們的理由是；生活中碰到難題，可以第一時間找到吾，並給於他們實際的幫助。這些客人有這樣的想法，是真的可以理解的，或許他們忘了，「天下無不散之宴席」，這句話。

　　人與人之間的因緣，是非常之微妙的，又不可思議的。不是嗎？想想看，最疼愛妳、你的人，現在還在妳、你身邊嗎？最要好的同學，如今是否還有聯絡？最敬愛的師長，還在嗎？幼時的玩伴，現在在哪裡？人生是要順應變遷的，更要在這人事因緣變遷中，學習獨立、學習堅強、啓發智慧、累積經驗，未來才能更上一層樓。

　　曾有人要求吾守護他一家人，一直到其子女長大成人，他敢講吾倒是不敢聽。哈！哈！哈！其實啊！到今天依然有男有女，一樣要吾守護他們一家人，長長久久，祇是有些是明說，有些則眼神透露，確實叫吾受寵若驚，一時不知如何回應。這時才領悟，什麼叫有情眾生。說真的，每當有這些客人的請求，吾都是感到無比榮幸的，祇是君子之交淡如水啊！有緣自然來相聚，互相珍惜，惜福惜緣，那就夫復何求了。

　　我們「出現」在這人世間，只有兩個字，那就是修行，修正我們的行為，一直到達覺行圓滿，永遠快樂、自在、任運，這種眞實的覺受境界，唯有眞正成佛才能夠完完全全體會及擁有。吾少食少眠少憩，就是爲了你們的「終生大事」，除此之外，吾已找不到任何意義寫作。親愛的讀者粉絲們，切記師父引進門，修行在個人。

英譯

Many years ago, some clients told me that they wanted to buy a residential unit near my place, a unit as near as possible! At that time, I had to be like the ninja as depicted in the movie, moving around stealthily to prevent myself from being discovered! Their reason to live near me was to have immediate access to my practical assistance, should they encounter problems in life. I can totally understand why my clients think this way but perhaps they forget that all good times must come to an end.

The affinity between people is very intricate and unfathomable. Is it not so? Think about it, the one who doted on you most, is he or she by your side now? The best of classmates, are you still in touch with them now? The teacher whom you respected the most, is he or she still around? Your playmates from childhood, where are they now? Our lives are always in a constant flux of change. In the midst of all these changes in our relationships, we should learn to be independent and strong, develop our own wisdom and accumulate our experience. Only then can we make progress.

Once, there was a person who requested me to watch over his entire family, until his children grow up. It was an audacious request that I could not bear to hear. Ha ha ha! In fact, even till today, there are still such requests from my clients, some verbal, others through their eye expressions, to look after their families. I am taken aback by these requests and the trust bestowed on me, that I do not know how to react at first. It was at such a moment that the realisation hit me: sentient beings are emotional creatures. Every time I hear such a request, I am honoured, but the friendship between men of virtue should be pure like water and free from self-interest. We will meet and gather when the conditions arises, and we should treasure one another and our affinity. Only then will we have no regrets.

We appear in this world for a singular purpose: spiritual cultivation. That is to cultivate righteousness in our speech, body and mind and attain enlightenment, achieving eternal bliss, freedom and contentment. Only beings in the state of Buddhahood are able to fully experience this state of Truth. I compromised on my sleep and meal times to prepare you for the "biggest event of your life". There is no other goal

more worthy than that for me to continue my writings. My beloved readers, please keep in mind that a Master can only show you the door, you will have to take the first step in.

修福惜福
Cultivate and Treasure Your Merits

　　近期堪察陽宅地理，批八字及教課，累積好些感觸。先談談堪察陽宅地理方面的的感觸吧！吾受邀爲一對夫婦尋找適合他們命掛的商店，好讓他們能夠在「黃昏」之前，少造「黑業」多造「白業」。可是，看了三處，不只風水方面不佳，當中也顯現他們「福元」的指數，以及佛所說的，業力不可思議啊！

　　批八字有批大運、批流年兩種。大運是指從出生到晚年。流年則是十二個月的運程分析與規劃。批八字的感觸是，有些人將要面臨「山窮水盡」，卻依然固執己見、任意妄爲、好逸惡勞、得過且過、騙人騙己等等，顯然將吾所給於的指點拋出腦後，選擇棄明投暗，再不趕緊棄暗投明，未來一定應驗吾所推斷的，這樣又何必浪費時間與金錢來找吾批算呢？更又爲何尋苦，而不尋樂呢？此謂癡哉、癡哉。咎由自取，自做自受。

　　教課方面，是學生們的明知故犯。新的一批學生，吾先教戒律及禮儀以正其心、以正其行，以期早日覺行圓滿，眞正離苦得樂。但目前爲止，他們還是我行我素，根本就沒有學佛的正確心念、正確精神，這樣下去是危險的，最終學佛不成，變成學魔，豈不哀哉。愼之，愼之。

　　眞的有好些人日盼夜盼，盼能遇逢大善知識，或善知

識，引領他們出苦輪，可是兩鬢雙白都盼不到。如今你們已遇逢之，卻又將他給「推走」，有福無福，可見一般。無論有福無福，勸君修福惜福，「過了這一村，就沒有這間店了」。珍重。

There were many after thoughts and feelings recently on my recent sessions of Feng Shui audits, destiny analysis and teaching lessons. Well, let me first share with you my after thoughts from my Feng Shui audits! A couple engaged me to evaluate the locations of several shop lots for their business, based on the suitability of their birth charts. I was hoping that before their lives enter into the "sunset" phase, they would get to do more good in their line of work than now. However, after viewing the three different locations, not only did they have poor Feng Shui, it was evident that the merit level of this couple was low. What Buddha has taught us, that the power of Karma is inexplicable, was well and truly reflected in this episode.

Destiny analysis can be categorised them into 2 components: a macro and comprehensive analysis of your whole life and a detailed breakdown of your twelve-month luck cycle in a particular year. What I felt deeply in this aspect is some people are almost at the end of the road but he or she still obstinately hangs on to their self-deceiving unwholesome thoughts and actions without any remorse or repent. They are indolent and totally disregarded my advice to them, choosing to remain in Darkness rather than to walk on the Path of Light. It will be too late if they do not pull up their socks now, as they will end up just like how I had predicted they would be. If that is the case, why waste time and money to seek my advice? Why do they seek sufferings instead of happiness? This is ignorance indeed. They have to reap what they sow.

Speaking about my Dharama lessons, I have observed the willful transgression of the students. For my current batch of students, I focus my teachings on the precepts and decorum, with the aim of inculcating the right morals in them. Having the right mindset will translate into correct actions and this will set them on the path towards Enlightenment and liberation from mortal sufferings. Alas, they are still very much unrepentant and persistent in their old ways of doing things. They lack the correct mindset and spirit in learning the Dharma and it is very dangerous if this continues, as they may well be on the path of the Devil, instead of the Dharma. Beware!

It is true that there are many people out there who pine day and night to meet a highly attained master to lead them out of this cycle of suffering, but they never get to meet one

even after their hair turn white. Now you have found one such master and yet you pushed him away. It is evident how much merits you truly have. Regardless of your merits, heed my advice to cultivate diligently and treasure your merits. As the Chinese saying goes, "Once you have passed this village, you may not find what you are looking for in the next one."

Take care, my friend.

借你呆看幾十年
Just For Your Viewing Pleasure

　　妳、你快樂嗎？妳、你真的快樂嗎？妳、你開心嗎？妳、你真的開心嗎？妳、你悲傷嗎？妳、你憂愁嗎？無論快樂或悲傷，無論開心或憂愁，妳、你可會認認真真的靜下心來想一想，這些「覺受」都是和我們，形影不離、同生同死的。那既然是如此，我們又何必去執著這些與生俱來的「覺受」而讓它們變成我們心靈昇華的障礙呢？

　　親愛的諸位大德，玳瑚師父閱人無數，發現很多很多人還沒快樂，還沒自在。這當然跟他們不懂得「借你呆看幾十年」有關。金錢、名位、地位、女色、豪宅、名車等等，或許在妳、你眼中、心中，這「媚影」常揮之不去，那是因為妳、你還未有「明空的智慧」，不曉得妳、你眼中、心中的這些「媚影」，一不留神，將讓妳、你名譽掃地、斷送前程，最終還有可能倒地不起。

　　有人為了金錢，寧願不顧自己親生骨肉，去買較便宜的嬰兒車，差點導致其嬰孩「倒地不起」。有人貪睡，屢次遲到慈善活動。有人不守戒律，叛離自己的師父。有人辛勤工作竟然是為了圓其不著邊際的「虛榮心」。有人死守那最終都不屬他的「石頭」（名錶、金錶、金、銀、珠寶）。要認清這些真的是身外物，這些面子、「石頭」、名位、地位等等，就是無形的枷鎖，無形的繩子，必須當機立斷的看破及

放下。要不然,它一定將妳、你綁的死死,絕無可能讓妳、你快樂自在。

　　親愛的諸位大德、粉絲及讀者,玳瑚師父常聽到你們心中叫喊著;我要自由、我要快樂。若你們一天不認清這些「假相」,你們就不可能等到自由與快樂的那一天到來。「面子」、名位、地位、「石頭」、美貌、身段,等等,在智者的眼中,祇是「借妳、你呆看幾十年」而已。

───── 英譯 ─────

Are you happy? Are you really happy? Are you feeling joyous? Are you really feeling joyous? Or do you feel sad and sorrowful? Regardless if you are feeling happy or sad, joyous or sorrowful, have you ever given it a serious thought that these emotions are always with us, very much like our own shadows? If that is so, why do we hold on tightly to these innate emotions and allow them to obstruct our psychological progression?

My dear readers, Master Dai Hu has read countless people and discovered that many of them have not found their happiness and peace. The cause of it boils down to the fact that they have not realised that their worldly possessions are only temporal. Perhaps to you, the allure of wealth, fame,

183

status, women, luxurious residences and cars, etc, may be hard to shake off. That is because the wisdom has not arisen in you to see through the illusion, that these things are only temporal. If you are not careful, your attachment to worldly possessions can tarnish your fame and destroy your future, in some cases with no respite at all.

There was a person who bought a cheaper baby pram so as to save some money, resulting in the child incurring a fall. There was another person, whose craving for more sleep, resulted in him being late several times for charity events. There was yet another person who did not adhere to the precepts and walked out on his teacher. Some people worked tirelessly just to satisfy their unrealistic vanity dreams. Some would guard over a "rock" that would never belong to them. By "rock", I am referring to material possessions like luxurious watches, gold watches, gold, silver, and precious stones. We must recognise that these possession never truly belong to us, and they are like invisible locks on us. We must decisively break these locks of attachments before they tighten their grip on us and making it impossible to achieve happiness and peace.

My dear readers, Master Dai Hu often hear the cries from your heart, "I yearn for freedom, I want happiness." If you

are not able to see clearly the illusions of life, you will never taste true freedom and happiness. In the eyes of the wise and enlightened ones, fame, social status, the "rocks", good looks, physical figures, etc, are only for your gawking for just that few decades.

真正的有錢人
A Truly Wealthy Person

　　妳、你有看過有錢人嗎？妳、你身邊有有錢人嗎？妳、你心目中有錢人的定義或準則，是不是住豪華洋房，駕大房車，抽雪茄，有幾位傭人，是大公司的董事長，大企業家，好幾個老婆，等等？如果這些眞是妳、你心目中有錢人的定義或準則的話，那妳、你就非常有必要，從這篇文章中，吸取正確的知見，以免墮入他們「千方百計」的計劃中。

　　記得年少時曾問父親，爲何有錢人（做老闆的），總是比較「節約」？父親的回答是：就是因爲他們「節約」，才能成爲老闆啊！那時的吾是同意父親的，但學佛法，參佛法，在因緣因果的深意裡，吾得到了更圓滿的答案。有些有錢人他們在家中，吃粥配罐頭，如水仙牌蘑菇、五香肉丁、三個A菜心罐、四川腐乳，等等。他們錢財有進無出，等等。

　　當然，省吃儉用也算是一種美德。但他們並不是沒有能力，購買較健康的食物啊！錢財有進無出，儲蓄當然也是一種好習慣。可是，吃了不健康的食物，老來身體病痛多多，把所有或大部份的錢，都花在醫藥上，最後也變成沒有錢。大半輩子所賺來的錢，存在銀行，不捨得花，也不捨得捐出去做慈善公益，這些錢是屬於銀行，不是屬於妳、你的啊！是銀行富有，而並非妳、你富有啊！到頭來，妳、你其實是

乞丐，而不是什麼有錢人啊！

眞正的有錢人，是懂得賺錢，也懂得及捨得花錢的。桌上的一碗飯，妳、你祇看沒吃，這碗飯由始至終，根本不屬於妳、你的。妳、你有一百萬，可是妳、你從來都未曾花過半分錢，這一百萬，由始至終，也根本不屬於妳、你的。

───── **英譯** ─────

Have you seen a rich person before? Do you have any such person in your social circle? What is your definition of a wealthy person? Is it one who lives in a luxurious bungalow? Or drive a big limousine? Or smoke cigars? Or has several servants? Is it one who holds directorship in a big company? A great entrepreneur? Or a man with several wives etc? If the above conditions are your definition of wealth, then you really need to read on, to absorb the right knowledge and not fall into a well-designed trap.

I remembered asking my Dad a question when I was a child. I asked him why rich people (the businessmen) were thrifty in nature. He replied that it was this virtue of thrift that enabled them to accumulate wealth. At that time, I agreed with his view. However, after I learnt the Dharma and contemplated on it, I found a more complete answer in the profound meaning of karma and affinity. There are some rich people who ate simply for their meals like a bowl of porridge with canned food like Narcissus brand mushroom, spicy pork cubes, AAA brand pickled lettuce and Sichuan fermented bean curd etc. They accumulate their wealth but never give them away.

Of course, being thrifty is a virtue. But these people can well afford a more nutritious diet. Accumulating wealth and saving it is a good habit, but the poor diet they eat is going to cost them their health. As a result, as they aged, sickness befalls them, and they end up broke after spending their savings on medical bills. A lifetime of hard-earned wealth kept in the bank and not using it to do good only meant that these money belong to the bank and not you! It is the banks who are rich, not you! In the end, you are a beggar, not a wealthy man!

A truly wealthy person knows how to earn money, knows how to spend it, and is willing to spend it without being miserly. A bowl of rice on the table does not belong to you if you only merely look but not eat it. If you have a million dollars but do not spend a single cent of it, then right from the beginning, the money has never really belong to you at all.

真正的君子
The True Gentleman

常言道：君子有所爲，有所不爲。心胸寬廣、行事光明磊落、敢做敢當、懺悔己過、感恩圖報、改過遷善，等等。這些謂爲君子所爲。喜射暗箭、胡做非爲、不明事理、恩將仇報、過河拆橋、癲三倒四、明知故犯、棄善從惡，等等。這些謂爲君子不爲。一件事情還沒弄清楚，道聽途說、人云亦云、以外貌取人、先入爲主……這樣也非佛弟子、君子所爲。信因果明因果是我們佛弟子及君子行事之準則。這點不可不知啊！

親愛的諸位大德，請靜下心來仔細想：當今世上，有誰能天天筆耕，寫書兩百四十多本（仍然在寫），發願粉身碎骨渡眾生，且最後一位成佛、天天修法從無一日間斷、每星期六上法座，主持法會及佛法開示、法會後還爲世界各地萬千佛弟子摩頂，等等。吾的根本傳承上師，南無蓮生活佛，就是一位如此眞修行，眞行願的眞正的活佛。祂是吾心中不折不扣，眞正的君子。

—— 英譯 ——

As the saying goes, "A gentleman should conduct himself in honourable ways." Having an encompassing heart, be perfectly open and above board in his actions, being courageous and taking responsibility for his deeds and repent for his misdeeds, being grateful and seek to repay the kindness, being genuine in changing oneself for the better, etc, these are honourable conduct model of a true gentleman, a man of noble character.

On the other hand, traits like stabbing another in his back, committing misdeeds, being unreasonable, repaying kindness with vengeance, being an ingrate to your benefactors, distorting the truth, transgressing willfully, choosing the path of evil over good etc, are not exemplary of a true gentleman. Similarly, if you form an opinion without investigating the facts, relying on hearsay, following the herd despite its flaws, judging something by appearance and having preconceived notions, such behaviour are not desirable for a Buddhist and a true gentleman. To believe and understand the Law of Karma is a code of conduct for all Buddhists and true gentlemen. This is something we must all know!

To all beloved and virtuous readers, please still your heart and ponder deeply on this: in this current era, who can keep writing day after day, with over two hundred forty book titles under His name (and still writing till today), and make a vow to deliver all sentient beings even if it means crushing His bones and breaking His body to pieces, before attaining Buddhahood? Who can persevere with His daily

spiritual practice continuously, preside over puja ceremonies and give Dharma sermons every Saturday, and make the extra effort to grant blessings on the heads of thousands of disciples from all over the world, after the puja ceremonies? My Root Guru Master, Namo Living Buddha Lian Sheng, is one true Living Buddha who truly practices and truly lives His vows. In my heart, without a single doubt, He is the perfect true gentleman.

真愛新春佳節
My Truly Beloved Spring Festival

舊歲新歲且莫醉
羊年行善不可退
身強體健為之最
諸事亨通當守戒

　　心中有幾個節日，是吾喜歡及期待的。吾也悄悄地在自心中，有個所謂的排行榜，而排名第一的，也是吾唯一「引頸期待」的，就是新春佳節。這麼多年來，吾都是默默地、專一地、耐心地、等候它的到來。新春顧名思義，就是冬去春來，四季復始，萬象更新，是另一年美好的開始，舊年裡來不及完成的事與願，就在新的一年裡，再接再厲地去完成，及圓滿它。

　　新年新氣象的氣，指的是好的氣場，好的磁場。怎樣能納得好的氣場，和好的磁場呢？欲要納得好的氣場，妳、你就必須得勤快地整理及規劃妳、你的居家。至於好的磁場，妳、你就得確保，妳、你的心情指數，常在「健康水平」。哈！哈！哈！這是屬內的。外的是妳、你身上所穿的、戴的、提的，等等。更細地說，就是妳、你所穿的、戴的、提的、塗抹的，的品牌及設計圖案，一定要符合妳、你先天八字的喜用神。這樣就叫除舊迎新、祥瑞連年。讚！

向上善

　　玳瑚師父真愛新春佳節，也是因爲春節乃唯一，直接、清晰、快速，給予吾「感應」的節日。它那「新」的、旺的、祥和的磁場，就是那麼直接地來報曉，當春風吻上吾的臉時，勉勵吾舊年裡，所有不愉快的人與事，已經隨著舊年告個段落了。新的希望、新的展望，已在吾的手中，隨時隨刻，發光發熱。讚！

　　玳瑚師父溫馨提醒大家，春節家中必備的東西，要有年花、汽水、水果、八寶盒、年糕、發糕、年柑、等等。除夕團圓飯，可千萬別吃粥啊！團圓飯應豐盛些，因爲，那是確定妳、你來年「豐不豐盛」的。祝笑呵呵，樂團圓。

英譯

Be it the past year or the new year, do be sober,
In the Year of Goat, keep up with the virtuous deeds,
Make your health and spiritual well-being your top priority,
Even when all goes well, do not forget your precepts.

In my heart, there are a few festivals that I especially like and look forward to. I secretly ranked these festivals and the number one favorite, the one that had me eager with anticipation, is none other than the Spring Festival (Chinese New Year). All these years, I have always waited quietly, patiently and faithfully for the Spring Festival to arrive. As the name implies, this festival heralds the end of winter, the arrival of spring and the start of the four seasons. It signifies the renewal of all things, the start of another beautiful year. All unfulfilled ambitions and uncompleted tasks from the past year are set for completion and fulfillment in this new year.

"New Year, New Hope" points out the presence of good energies and auras. How do we usher in these good energies and auras? To receive the good energies, you need to diligently tidy and organize the space in your home. As for the good auras, it all starts with you keeping your emotions at a healthy level. Ha! Ha! Ha! This is about the internal workings of your own self. As for the external works, we are talking about the clothes and accessories that you wear, etc. To be more precise, they are the clothes you put on, bags that you carry, cosmetics that you apply, as well as the brand and the overall design. They must be aligned to the favourable elements in your birth chart. This is what I call a total renewal-getting rid of the old to receive the new, for a prosperous and auspicious year ahead! Bravo!

Another reason why Master Dai Hu is so fond of the Spring Festival (Chinese New Year) is because this is the only festival that gives me a direct, clear and swift indication of its energies of renewal, prosperity and harmony. As the winds of Spring caress my face, it seems to encourage me that the unhappiness from the past year had came to a close.

In this New Year, I am already holding new hopes, new prospects in my hands, ever ready to shine brightly. Bravo!

During this Spring festival, here is a gentle reminder of the list of essentials every household should have: New Year flowers, soft drinks, fruits, new year sweets in a hexagonal box, New Year cake (Nian gao), Fortune cake (Fa gao), mandarin oranges, etc. During the reunion dinner, avoid consuming porridge! The reunion dinner should be sumptuous as this determines if you will have a bountiful harvest in the coming year. Wishing everyone a year of hearty laughter and blissful reunions.

真實的現象
The True Reality

　　吾看人很快。一個人走過吾的身邊，吾就能夠知道這個人到底有幾兩。有錢沒錢、有實力沒實力，絕對騙不了吾。

　　以前上課時，有些徒弟常拿別人的照片來問吾意見，如可不可以和某人合作、某人的病可會痊愈、某人的婚姻可有救等等，大家因為吾的準而問的不亦樂乎，也學了不少。弟子對吾的相術讚嘆不已。客人也多次帶照片請吾指點他們該雇用哪位女傭、可否和某人交往或合夥等。

　　吾從照片看相快，看真人也一樣快。有些人來到吾面前裝可憐，說自己如何沒錢，又或者說自己如何是個專一的丈夫等，都會一一被吾說破，甚至斥罵。吾不喜歡撒謊的人，所以請不要在吾面前班門弄斧。

　　最近，吾指點一位婦女。她脾氣暴躁、喜占便宜、禮貌不好、眼神不善、性格固執、手腳不乾淨，太多太多的缺陷了。吾不但看到她不光彩的過去，更看到她不好的未來。她的樣子一臉病容，開始脫髮，吾知道她將來很可能會患癌。

　　可憐嗎？但一切都是自己造成的，怨不得人。

　　吾看到了，但吾沒有說出來。因為做師父的，不能說恐嚇的話。這也是吾做師父的難。不講真的，又說吾不準。要如何講才能取悅客人，真是一門大學問。

　　吾為她難過，頻頻提醒她要改過的地方，希望她能夠在

禍還未臨時，速速將習性除掉，但不得要領。講的越直，她越是不看著吾說話，眼神更不悅。

如此一來，吾更無法向她說了。有時，吾也希望有看不準的時候。

─── 英譯 ───

My observation of people is fast. When a person walks past me, I am able to know the weight of his fortune. Whether he is wealthy or not, whether he is capable or not, it is impossible to escape my eyes.

During my lessons, some of my disciples would show me photographs of people and asked me questions. Is this person a good business partner? Is this person able to recover from his illness? Can the marriage of this person be saved? Delighted at my accuracy, the students had much learning fun and were in awe of my expertise in face reading. Clients have, on numerous occasions, showed me photos and seeked my advice on the suitable choice of a maid, a love partner or business partner.

I am quick in physiognomy via photos and just as efficient in reading a person in real life. Some people come to me, giving sob stories of their poor financial state, while some men speak of their steadfast loyalty to their wives. I saw through them very soon and gave them a dressing down. I do not appreciate liars, so please do not put up a show in front of me.

Recently, I gave advice to a lady. She had too many undesirable traits. She was foul-tempered and obstinate, took advantage of others' kindness, had sticky fingers and poor manners with much unkindness in her eyes, just to name a few. Not only do I saw her wretched past, I also saw the bleak future to come for her. Her face was one of sickness and has obvious signs of hair loss. I knew she will be besieged with cancer in time to come.

Was she pitiful? But it was all her own doing. She had no one to blame but herself.

I saw all these but I did not tell her. As a Master, I refrain from frightening others with my predictions. What a dilemma for me sometimes! If I do not speak the truth, my predictions will be deemed inaccurate. It is indeed an art of the speech to please the client in such a situation.

I felt sad for her, and repeatedly reminded her to change her ways, hoping that she would rid her bad habits before disaster strikes. However, my advice felt on deaf ears. The more honest I was in pointing out her flaws, the more she looked away from me during conversation, with

intensifying displeasure in her eyes.

It is now even more difficult for me to tell her the truth. Sometimes I wish I am inaccurate in my reading too.

財源廣進
Wealth and Prosperity Abound!

　　財源廣進是生意人，很喜歡的一句吉祥語及話。當然不只是做生意的人，而是人人皆喜愛。尤其在春節期間，很多人都喜在公司或家裡，貼上這句超級敬愛的吉祥賀詞，祇因財為養命之物。很多很多人，都會奔向廟宇，向佛菩薩神明禱之、求之，願財源廣進，這些是無可厚非的。玳瑚師父是希望，這樣的朋友們，能夠智慧增長，要不然就會入籍迷信。

　　迷信或不迷信，差別在於智慧之有無。怎麼說呢？那你們認真想想看，為何有人一求就有，為何有人求了良久，始終不得要領？這當中不關佛菩薩、老天爺及神明的事。這當中關係到求的人，福份的次第，以及因緣因果。所謂財源廣進，是指妳、你要先有進財之源，而且是多方面的進財之源。之後自然有源源不斷的財，湧進妳、你的口袋。

　　上段所述的，是清楚地教導大家，離開迷信，歸向正信，也是有理智地納財，真正的財源廣進。所以從現在開始，不要放過任何行善的機會，哪怕是做義工、哪怕是勸善、哪怕是免費幫人家搬家，不過這必須得有人請，白天而不是夜裡，那就不是小偷了。哈！哈！哈！

　　記得哦！佛菩薩、老天爺及神明，賜財賜福，是因求的人，常行善布施、戒殺放生、孝順父母、禮敬師長、奉公守

法，等等。這些善行即是財來之源，千萬不可背道而馳啊！若是妳、你還是不知從何開始，歡迎妳、你到來向吾討教，妳、你若學會，保證財源廣進。

The auspicious Chinese phrase "Wealth and Prosperity Abound" is one which all businessmen love to hear. Of course, its popularity is not limited to the business owners, in fact, this phrase is a hot favourite among everybody. Especially during the Spring Festival period, this extremely well-liked phrase will be written on red couplets and pasted in homes and offices. All because money is a mean of life preservation. Inevitably, many people would flock to the temples and pray feverntly to the Buddhas and Bodhisattvas for wealth and prosperity. Master Dai Hu hopes that these people will grow in wisdom and not fall into the trappings of myths and superstitions.

Whether something is superstition or not depends on if there is any logical wisdom in it. Why do I say that? Think about this: why are there some people who get their wishes granted as soon as they pray for it, while there are others whose prayers seem to fall on deaf ears, despite repeated praying? This has absolutely nothing to do with the Buddhas, Bodhisattvas and Gods. It has everything to do with the amount of merits of the person making the prayer, as well as karmic and conditional implications. To even begin to have "wealth and prosperity abound", you need to create the source of wealth and prosperity, and we are not talking about just one single source. With more sources you have, there will naturally be a steady flow of wealth and prosperity pouring into your pockets.

The above paragraph serves to educate everyone to have the right mindset, move away from the myths and superstitions, and accumulate wealth in a logical manner to truly prosper. Thus from this moment onwards, do not let loose any chance, however trivial it may seem, to do good. Be it volunteering your time, dispensing good moral advice, or helping someone move house free of charge. For the latter, you must of course be asked to do so at the request of the owner before moving his things. If you do it at night without any invitation, that will make you a burglar! Ha ha ha!

Remember this, the Buddhas, Bodhisattvas, the Heavens and deities dispense wealth and fortune to a person based on the amount of merits he or she accumulated from virtuous deeds such as abstinence from killing, show of filial piety, show of respect and obedience to teacher and elders, adherence to the law and order of society, etc. These are the true sources of your wealth and prosperity. Do not go

against these! If you have no inkling on how to even begin, you are most welcome to seek advice from me. Once you have learnt the way, it is definitely going to be "Wealth and Prosperity abound"!

健康在陰陽
Being Healthy is about Yin & Yang

　　來到吾前的客人，約有九十巴仙「身心」都不健康，這麼多年來，這現象不只沒有改善，反而越來越不「明朗」。身爲修行人、玄學家，且近日常告知人們吾也是醫生的我，十分關注這日見嚴重的問題，於是決定俯案筆耕，將這萬金難買的「健康要訣」，免費大放送。願有緣觀讀的妳、你，不要等閒視之，也不要進入寶庫，卻空手回啊！

　　中西醫學理論，至今依然沒有達成共識，是有跡可尋的。吾玳瑚師父，是較提倡中華醫學理論的。原因在於中華醫學，有最自然的原理，那就是陰陽五行。要知道，天上五星到人體裡，就是心、肝、胃、肺、腎，到食物就是咸、酸、苦、甜、辛。而陰陽在飲食方面，冷飲爲陰，熱飲爲陽，未煮的水爲陰，煮過的水爲陽，白飯爲陰，炒飯爲陽，鮮奶及豆奶爲陰，咖啡爲陽。陰陽在日常生活中，睡覺爲陰，工作爲陽，睡太多會出事，睡太少也不妙，不睡早晚要出事。哈！哈！哈！

　　中華醫學是我們偉大的祖先，親身試藥、耐心觀察「天相」、季節變換，才寫出「歷久不衰」的醫學巨著。西方醫學就是沒有這陰陽五行的概念，所以出錯的機會較多。激光掃描、抽骨髓及動手術，是很多人「吃不消」的，很多人也因爲這樣，提前「移民」了。雖然，或許中藥療效慢，但慢

並不代表不會痊癒啊！這點大家必須認真思考。

　　相信觀讀吾寫的這篇文章的妳、你，已經知曉人為何會生病的原因了。是的，那是陰陽不調，及不懂自己應攝取的五行食物。如果妳、你還是不清楚的話，不大緊，吾再傳授妳、你，簡單有效的方法使自己健康。方法是多看大自然、多幫助他人、每天起床對著鏡子微笑，不說妳、你不知，憂愁為陰，快樂為陽哦！

　　祝：健康。

───── 英譯 ─────

Around 90% of the clients I saw are in an unhealthy state, both in body and mind. It has been a worrying trend all these years with no sign of it abating. As a spiritual practitioner, a Chinese Metaphysicist as well as a doctor, I view this trend seriously. Thus I have decided to share a secret to good health, a secret that is worth more than a thousand taels of gold, for the price of nothing! I wish for those with affinity to read this article not to view it as ordinary and go off empty-handed.

Till present, there has not been any commonality between Traditional Chinese Medicine (TCM) and its Western counterpart. I advocate the theories and applications of TCM. The main reason being that TCM theories are aligned with the Nature, which encompasses Yin and Yang, and the five elements. You need to know that the five Heavenly Stars in our body are represented by our Heart, Liver, Spleen, Lungs and Kidneys. In our food, the five elements are seen in Saltiness, Sourness, Bitterness, Sweetness, Spiciness. As for the Yin and Yang in our food, cold is Yin, hot is Yang. Unboiled water is Yin, boiled water is Yang. Steamed rice is Yin, fried rice is Yang. Fresh milk and soy milk are Yin, coffee is Yang. In our daily lives, sleep is Yin, work is Yang. Too much of sleep will create issues whereas too little sleep is not ideal either. If you do not sleep at all, it is only a matter of time before you get into trouble! Ha ha ha!

Traditional Chinese Medicine originated from our forefathers, who tried and tested it with their bodies and through mindful observation of the heavens and seasonal changes, to produce this noble body of knowledge that withstood the trials of time. Western medicine does not have the concept of Yin and Yang, and the five elements, and hence, a higher probability for errors. Not many people can withstand the stress of these western treatments like MRI scan, bone marrow transplant, and intrusive surgeries, and as a result, passed away prematurely. Even though TCM has a slower effect, that does not imply the treatment is ineffective. This point deserves a serious think through.

I believe those of you who read this article would have

known by now the reason we fall sick. Yes, it is due the imbalance of Yin and Yang and improper food intake due to the ignorance of our favorable elements. If you are still in the dark, fret not, for I will impart you a simple method for a healthy you. It is simply to see more of the nature, to be generous in helping people, to smile at yourself in the mirror every morning u get out of bed. Do not say that you did not hear me: To be gloomy is Yin, to be happy is Yang!

Wishing good health to all.

唱首情歌給妳、你聽
Singing A Love Song For You

　　妳、你若是吾忠實的粉絲或讀者，妳、你必然曉得，吾在大約十五年前，就以佛法及玄學，沿家挨戶同步利樂諸有情，為期兩年左右。近千日的利生歲月裡，累積了足已寫成萬篇短暫人生的情議故事，因此，吾就很自然地將這篇文章，題名為〈唱首情歌給妳、你聽〉，惟願這沒曲調的「情歌」，能牽動「六神無主」的妳、你，邁向永恆快樂、光明的未來境界，而不至於墮落那淒淒慘慘、慘慘淒淒的痛苦境界。

　　當年的某一天，吾來到北部的一戶人家，而迎接吾的，是一名婦女，吾分析其姓名吉凶後，就與其談及她的人生狀況，吾也就開門見山地問她，是否有過墮胎。她似乎沒有正面回答吾，吾就遞給她一張寫有吾聯絡電話的小卡片，事後就繼續沿家挨戶，利樂其他有情。夜晚返回居所，也沒把這件事情放在心頭。

　　隔了幾天，吾的手機響起，所顯示的號碼，並不是吾所識得的號碼，但吾還是接了。電話的另一端聲音，也顯得陌生，查問之後，原來是那位婦女。她承認吾之推算準確，及有水子靈的過失，但她告訴吾並不是手術墮胎的，而是在一次的如廁時，把嬰孩排出的，她跟著問吾該怎麼辦，吾叫她在某個日子來找吾，吾會有辦法教於她，可是她卻沒有赴

約。

　吾，玳瑚師父，在此奉勸所有胎死腹中、人工墮胎、如廁排出、生出但幾天或幾月就死的（夭折），等等，都是會懷著恨意，而其父母日後必定會有諸多不順，在家庭、事業、健康、生意、子女等等方面。請反問你自己，若有人沒經過妳、你同意，就將妳、你生命立刻取走，妳、你會怎麼樣？快快請教高明之士吧！這業障不會祇是一世啊！

―― 英譯 ――

If you are one of my loyal readers and fans, you would surely know that I began my journey of propagating the Dharma and Chinese metaphysics, to benefit sentient beings almost fifting years ago, going door to door for around two years or so. Through the years (I counted almost a thousand days!), I have accumulated enough real-life encounters to pen down tens of thousands of stories, depicting the trials and tribulations of the short-lived human life. That is why I titled this article as Singing A Love Song For You, hoping that this special song, with no musical tune to go with it, will attract those of you who are not yet master of your own fate, encourage you to tread the path of eternal bliss and light, and not fall into the abyss of despair, pain and sufferings.

During the early years, I remembered one day when I visited a family in the north of Singapore. A lady received me, and after analyzing her name (and the good and bad associated with it), we chatted about other aspects of her life. I asked her frankly if she have had an abortion before but she did not give me a direct answer. Before I left to continue my rounds, I passed her my name card and forgot about our encounter when I returned home late that night.

A few days later, my mobile phone rang and I did not recognize the number on the caller ID display. I picked it up anyway. The voice on the other end sounded unfamiliar as well. After some clarification, she turned out to be the lady whom I met. She admitted I got it correct, that she had an abortion before. She told me that it was not a surgical abortion, but the fetus was discharged from her body while she was in the toilet. She asked for my advice, and I told her to meet me on a certain day to hear my solution. Alas, she did not turn up for our appointment.

In all seriousness, Master Dai Hu would want to highlight that the aborted child, be it through surgery or accident, even if the fetus died in the womb, or the newborn passed away within days or months of birth, would bear hatred for the parents who would be adversely affected in their family, career, health, business, descendants etc. Putting yourself in the shoes of the aborted child, how would you feel if

someone else took away your life without your permission? Act fast and consult a qualified person on this. This negative karma would last several lifetimes!

救人等同救己
Saving Others Is Akin To Saving Yourself

　　今年天災地難似乎特別多。本以爲這不過是自然界中的自然動態，可是這種動態怎麼每次都帶走這麼多人的生命？且被帶走的生命也好像一次比一次多。是時候我們人類應該放下各自的門戶之見，認眞地同心協力，爲我們的生存以及其它生命的生存，努力不懈的探討與研究如何或能否讓這些所謂的大自然動態減少再減少。

　　想來吾也太天眞了。自然界自有自然界的主宰，人類又憑什麼來與祂談條件？費了很大的勁兒想啊想，唯一能與自然界的主宰談條件的方法就是我們人類要眞心誠意的表現給祂看，給祂知道，我們珍惜所有的資源，我們尊重一切的生命。我們不會制造足以摧毀人的生命，一切生態之武器及軍火。我們互相尊重與和諧，我們敬天敬地……等等。

　　吾個人認爲最重要最重要的莫過於尊重一切生命。因爲有生命，佛性才能夠有機緣啓發，才能結束漫長的六道輪迴之苦啊！也就是因爲如此，萬萬不可以去墮胎啊！殺生的業最重，墮胎就是殺生啊！

　　若你們看到，聽到哪裡有災難，哪裡有人急需要幫忙，有錢出錢，有力出力。兩者皆可出，那當然是最棒。千萬不可「半點心」，要就全心全意。也只有全心全意才能夠發出最大的慈悲，讓自然界、罹難者，以及妳、你本身，感受眞

實的關愛。切記！救人等同救自己。

This year has seen many, more than it ought to be, natural disasters occurring. I originally thought this was just a natural phenomenon of Mother Nature. But why is this course of nature claiming more and more lives with every occurrence? It is about time that mankind lay down their biases against one another and work together seriously for the survival of not just mankind, but also all living beings. Mankind should strive relentlessly to find a solution to reduce the frequency of these calamities occurring.

213

I guess I am too naive. What right does mankind has to negotiate with Mother Nature, who is Her Own Master? I rack my brains exhaustively and concluded that probably the only way for us to talk terms with Mother Nature is for mankind to truthfully and sincerely show Her that we treasure all the natural resources and that we respect all life forms. We need to show Her that mankind is will give up making weapons of destruction that could cause countless deaths and destroy the ecological environment. We want to let Mother Nature know that we can respect one another and live together in harmony, and that we respect the Heavens and the Earth...... etc.

I personally feel that the most important of all is having respect for all lives. Because when given the opportunity to live, there is a chance that the Buddha Nature can be illuminated to finally end the sufferings in this long, long cycle of Samsara. That is why it is of utmost importance that you do not have abortion! Killing a life comes with a heavy karmic price to pay, and abortion IS killing life.

Should you see or hear of any disaster, or anyone in dire need of assistance, please do your part, in monetary terms or through your efforts. It would be excellent if you could do both. However, please do it with all your heart, not halfheartedly, for only when you give 100% would you evoke the greatest compassion for Mother Nature, the victims of the natural disasters and even your own self to feel the true care and concern.

清明時節談孝親
Filial Piety on Qingming Festival

清明時節雨紛紛，路上行人欲斷魂，
借問酒家何處有，牧童遙指杏花村。

美極的唐詩，用來揭開這妙美的文章，最是恰當不過
了。「妙」，妙在何處呢？妙在讓你們知道，人若無修行，
年輕時就可看出，她、他未來的「去向」。妙在讓你們知道
鬼神無所不在。妙在讓你們知道，人的呼吸之清濁，竟也決
定他們的未來「去向」啊！

在一次的「以茶會友」中，正忙於解說陽宅藍圖時，猛
然憶起其中一位來者的要求，故抬頭示意她可先回。她在現
實生活中，當然是不折不扣的人，可是那時呈現吾眼前的，
卻是一張「鬼臉」。隔了好幾天，又有因緣來向吾討教佛
法，吾就在用餐時，直言對她說。說出來是讓她快快，積極
地累積更深厚的福報，速將吾那時所看之「鬼臉」，轉化成
神臉、仙臉、菩薩臉，又或者佛臉，最起碼也要人臉吧！

一位一歲左右，就被一位沒有血緣關係的女子，含辛茹
苦撫養成人的男子，因女同事的介紹，來找吾批大運，從其
長相及八字，皆屬苦之一字。後來與他還有些緣分，就渡他
皈依佛門，願他善自珍重，學習善法達清淨。但吾早已看出
這人，乃財、色、名、食、睡，慾望重之人，所以對於他的

215

希望，也真的是那一點點的希望。吾相信不諳玄學的人，都會知道一位養育之恩未報，且還對養母的積蓄有貪念的人的後果是不明朗的。是的，這種人絕對有機會，過清明節。而前段述及的女子，有善知識特別為其教授佛法，苦口婆心又教又勸，大量光陰虛渡，自私又自利，所以其臉才現「鬼臉」，以示吾再勸之啊！

　　清明乃「水庫」之月份，清明時節雨紛紛，是不在話下的。是否所有冒雨上山掃墓的人兒，一定就是孝順的呢？又或者，上山掃墓是一種孝順的表徵呢？那如果答案是是的話，為何天色總是愁雲密佈，而沒有雨過天晴，愉悅之氣氛呢？記得讀小學時，有位男教師對我們說，孝順父母應在他們生前，而不是他們百年歸去後，才在他們墳前哭爸哭媽的。這位男教師所言極是。要知道不孝乃天地不容也。好壞皆有循環，何苦日後歷史重演，在妳、你身上呢？

―― 英譯 ――

The ceaseless rain drizzles like tears during Qing Ming,
So broken-hearted are the mourners on the way.
When asked where could a tavern be found,
A shepherd boy points to yonder village of the apricot flowers.

To start this interesting article with this beautiful poem from the Tang Dynasty is simply apt. Why is this article

fascinating? It tells you that if one does not cultivate spiritually, you can tell what the future beholds for him or her, even at a young age. It tells you of the omnipresence of the gods and spirits. It tells you that even the purity of our every breath determines our future path!

During one of the tea sessions, while I was busy explaining some Feng Shui pointers on a floor plan, I suddenly remembered a request from one participant, that she would like to leave the session early. I raised my head and signaled to her to leave first. What greeted me was a "ghostly" face, even though she is most certainly 100% human in real life. A few days later, the affinity arose as she came to learn the Dharma from me. During dinner, I told her straight what I saw the other day of her face, in hope that she would be diligent in accumulating merits and turn her life around quickly. I would like to see on her a face of the deity, celestial being, Bodhisattva or even the Buddha. At the very least, her face should look human!

I knew a man who was adopted, at the age of one. The lady, with totally no blood relation to him, brought him up painstakingly. He was introduced by a female colleague to look for me. I analyzed his birth chart, luck cycles as well as his facial features, and all pointed to one single outcome: suffering. In later days, we had some affinity and I guided him to take refuge in the Triple Gems and I wish him well that he would learn the great Dharma well, rid himself of all defilements and attain the state of purity. But I had long foretold that this person is a man of desires: wealth, lust, fame, gluttony and sloth, and thus I hold little hope, very little hope. I believe that even a person who is not familiar with the Chinese metaphysics would know that a person who has not repay his dues to his adopted mother for raising him up, and yet had greedy designs on her savings, would not have a good ending. The lady I mentioned in the above paragraph, despite having the affinity to meet a virtuous Buddhist practitioner who repeatedly teaches and advises her, squandered away a large part of her life and continued in her selfish ways. The "ghostly" face I saw was a sign to remind her again before it was too late!

The period of Qing Ming is the month of water storage, thus it is no wonder at all that there will be incessant rainfall during this time. Is it true that those, who braved the rain to visit the cemetery for tomb-sweeping, are certainly filial? Or is this act of tomb-sweeping a show of filial piety? If your answer is yes for both, why is the sky often gloomy and overcast, with no sun shining bright and cheery after the rain? I remembered a male teacher from my primary school days telling us that we should be filial to our parents while they were still alive, and not shed tears of anguish in front of their tombs after they had passed on? This male teacher was spot on. Please know that the Heaven and Earth will not

tolerate the unfilial ones, and what goes around comes around, be it the good or the bad. Is it worth it to see the bad history repeat itself in your life?

牽引你向道
Guiding You to the Way

近日勘察陽宅地理的感觸述之如下：

一、世人太不知「風水」的重要。
二、世人太不知因果之理。
三、世人太不知命。
四、世人太不知福元的次第。
五、世人太不知親近善知識。

人人都吶喊著要幸福，但卻從不安靜地坐下來，認真地思維如何才能真正的得到幸福。

上方所示之五點，若您能安靜、認真地思維，您朝思暮想的幸福，才能早日圓滿。

你我曾有同一夢，
曾幾何時夢非夢，
問吾是否已圓夢，
留偈一首助君夢。

I had the following sentiments after my recent Feng Shui audits:

1. The common people do not regard Feng Shui as important.
2. They have no knowledge on the Law of Karma.
3. They are not aware of their own destinies.
4. They do not understand what constitutes good fortune.
5. They do not appreciate and seek out wise and virtuous mentors.

Everyone is craving incessantly for happiness yet they never sit down in calmness and contemplate deeply on what it really takes to achieve happiness.

If you can quietly ponder the above five points in stillness and austerity, the true happiness you so yearn for day and night will be achieved sooner than you know.

We once had the same dream.
Since when did the dream become naught?
You ask if my dream has came true,
May this verse I leave help fulfill your dream.

被殺前的恐懼，您懂嗎？
Do You Know the Fear Before Being Killed?

那天經過樟宜機場日本餐館的魚缸時，吾依慣例地停下腳步。

幾天前，吾在此魚缸前爲水族念往生咒，今日再看，餐館進貨了，水族量明顯增加了。

魚缸裡面的水族都縮在一起，眼神都很恐慌、無助、絕望，全身軟綿綿，彷彿都已知道即將被宰殺的命運，縮在一起因爲誰都不想先被撈出水。

美食端上桌時，有多少食客會想到它們的恐懼呢？

吾提醒吾身旁的學生們，願眾生明白魚缸裡面的水族原本就是人。人這一世沒有修都很可能會變成魚缸裡面的水族。

人是高等的動物，應該有高等的智慧去想想這一世要如何解脫，而不是一味地吃喝玩樂。

在魚缸前，吾很用心地持往生咒，希望水族們能早日離苦得樂。

會念往生咒的佛友，可在用餐前持咒回向給這些畜類。

不會念的朋友們，可默念這往生短咒 7 遍或 21 遍回向：

往生淨土，

超生出苦，

南無阿彌陀佛。

南無阿彌陀佛。

南無阿彌陀佛。

戒殺是放生，肯持往生咒回向也是在放生。

如果這麼簡單都不肯念，那還算是善嗎？

會持此咒，一日行善的機會多得是。念念的善是要持續不斷才算是真善。

英譯

The other day as I passed by the fish tanks at a Japanese restaurant in Changi Airport, I came to a stop as per my usual habit.

Few days ago, I recited the Mantra for Rebirth in Pureland for the marine animals in these fish tanks. This day, the restaurant had new stocks and the quantity of the marine animals had visibly increased.

The marine animals in the fish tanks were all huddled together in a corner with fear, helplessness and hopelessness in their eyes. Their bodies seemed all lifeless, as if they already knew their inevitable destinies of being killed and took to huddling together, because no one wished to be the first to be fished out of the waters.

When the delicious dishes are being served on the table, how many people would think of the fear the animals experienced?

I told my students beside me of my hope that sentient beings would know the animals in the fish tanks were once human beings. If a person does not cultivate in this lifetime, there is a high possibility that one will reincarnate to be a aquatic animal.

Man is a supreme animal. We should have the supreme wisdom to ponder about liberation in this lifetime and not just indulge blindly in the worldly pleasures.

Standing in front of the fish tanks, I recited the Rebirth in Pureland Mantra diligently, praying that the marine animals can achieve liberation from this Samsara world.

Fellow Buddhist friends who know this mantra, do chant it before your meals and dedicate to the animals you are consuming.

If you do not know, you can recite this short version seven or twenty one times:
Short Mantra for Rebirth in Pureland

wǎng	shēng	jìng	tǔ		
往	生	淨	土		
chāo	shēng	chū	Kǔ		
超	生	出	苦		
nán	mó	ā	mí	tuó	fó
南	無	阿	彌	陀	佛
nán	mó	ā	mí	tuó	fó
南	無	阿	彌	陀	佛
nán	mó	ā	mí	tuó	fó
南	無	阿	彌	陀	佛

To abstain from killing is akin to freeing captive lives. Being willing to chant the Mantra for Rebirth in Pureland and dedicate the merits is also akin to freeing captive lives.

225

If one does not even wish to chant such a simple verse, how can one be considered kind?

If you know how to recite this mantra/verse, there are plenty of chances everyday for you to perform kind deeds. A truly kind person is one who continuously has kind and proper thoughts.

富與貧的學問
The Knowlededge Behind Wealth & Poverty

　　富與貧對吾來說，是先後的問題。怎麼說呢？就好比一位富甲一方的大富豪，為人驕傲又寒酸，平時的生活超節儉，吃粥陪三個A的荣心罐。這也並沒有甚麼不妥。問題是她、他從不布施。她、他也不善用這一世的財富，為下一世積累更深厚的福報。因此，這樣的富豪自然而然就沒有再富的因，來世也就自然而然不會再有富的果，不富反貧了。貧窮的這一世雖不富，但她、他很把握每一次行善的機會，久而久之，她、他也就脫離貧籍了。

　　另有一種是她、他都很積極做慈善與公益，可是邊做邊埋怨，也常常「碎碎唸」。這樣的行善法，也是無法與富結緣的。因為，所謂的行善，是要完完全全，歡喜甘願的去做的。吾這一說，諸位大德也應該有所領悟了。為何做了這麼多善事始終無法改善命運。還有一種是很喜歡占他人便宜的。這樣的人，當然也很難與富有緣。原因很簡單，她、他還沒積德，就先缺德了。真是「陰功」（廣東話）啊！不富的原因不只是這幾種。但這幾種是很要不得的，因為毫無善可言。我們若存著私心去行善，是有虧的。有虧，如何圓滿。一般人是無法察覺。但，鬼神是布滿十方法界的。人的念頭一起，鬼神早已知曉，無功反有過，命運祇會越來越凶啊！

行善是完全的給予，付出要有利人的心，不計較，持之以恆地去進行。歹運才能夠得以扭轉乾坤，反貧為富啊！好好學習這富與貧的學問吧！貧窮自然就會離妳、你遠遠的。玭瑚師父祝各位，願望早達。

--- 英譯 ---

In my opinion, being rich or poor is a matter of sequence. Why do I say that? Let's use an analogy of a extremely wealthy man who is a haughty scrooge. He leads a life of thrift, eating porridge with pickled vegetables all his life. There is nothing wrong with his lifestyle, except that he never once uses his wealth in this lifetime for the benefit of others and accumulate more merits for his next life. As such, in terms of the law of cause and effect, he did not create the seed or "cause" to be wealthy again in his next life. A person, who is poor this life, however recognizes and graps the opportunity to do good and accumulate merits often, he would plant the seed (cause) to be wealthy (effect) and break free from poverty eventually.

There is another kind of people who, despite his/her persistence in doing charity work, grumble non-stop as he/she is doing it. This behaviour or attitude would not have help their cause to accumulate merits for future fortune. Good deeds must be done willingly, with complete sincerity from the bottom of your heart. I hope with the above sentence, my dear readers would finally realise why, despite doing all the good deeds, there is no improvement to your lives.

There is yet another kind of people who love to take advantage of others. Such people would find it very difficult to have an affinity with wealth. Reason being, they are sorely lacking in virtues even before they accumulate more merits. How pathetic that is! No wonder good fortune and wealth do not come knocking at their doors.

There are many more reasons why a person is not wealthy this life, but the above mentioned are the significant ones to note and avoid. If we help others out of selfish motives, it will backfire on us in terms of karma. There is absolutely no kindness in such conduct. Like a round moon with a chip, it can never be full again. A layman will probably never realise but in the ten realms of existence are gods and spirits who are watching our every thought. Every unwholesome thought will lead us down the ill-fated path, further and further away from redemption.

To be able to give unreservedly is what I call doing good. This means giving yourself to benefit others, without being calculative, and to show perseverance to the end. Doing so would turn the tide in your life and let you make the leap

from poverty to wealth! Learn this wisdom well and poverty shall evade you naturally. I wish everyone an early fulfillment of your dreams!

最苦的人
The Person With The Most Sufferings

在你們的眼裡，怎樣的人會是你們認為，是世間最苦的人？是半身不遂的？是瞎眼的？是無家可歸的？是殘障的？是身無分文的？是失業的？是長相「麻麻地」的？還是⋯⋯？吾則認為，以上所問的，都不是世間最苦的人。世間最苦的人，莫過於有人無怨無悔，細心指導她、他，她、他始終還是選擇「飛蛾撲火」。這樣的人，就是世間最苦的人了。

人間不如意之事，本來就十之八九。但是在妳、你遇到這人生的瓶頸時，有位非常有能力的人，願意竭盡所能地，指引妳、你一條「峰迴路轉」的路，那這人生還是有甘味啊！

每個人本來就應為自己的命運負責。若妳、你有幸碰到，毫無條件帶妳、你走出那條漫長的崎嶇山路，何樂而不為呢？更何況，要碰到這樣的「真心英雄」，萬中難遇也。若妳、你僥倖遇之，無論如何都要將他留住，祇因他珍貴異常啊！

英譯

In your eyes, what kind of person do you think go through the most sufferings? Will he be someone who is paralyzed?

Or blind? Or homeless? Or physically disabled? Or penniless? Or jobless? Or one with a below average appearance? Or...? In my opinion, none of the above. I feel that the person who suffers the most is one who chooses a path of self-destruction, despite having someone by his or her side, painstakingly trying to provide a guiding light.

In this world, things often do not go our way, and it is only natural. However, at the juncture where you seemed to have hit an impasse, there is someone who has the ability and the willingness to guide you and turn things around, making it worthwhile after all!

Everyone of us should hold ourselves responsible for our own destiny. Should you have the good fortune to meet this person who can, unconditionally, lead you out of the long and windy road, will not it be a joyous thing? Furthermore, it will be down to divine luck in order for you to meet him or her, and you should try your very best to preserve this precious affinity, for he is so rare!

最靠近我們的神靈
The Deity Nearest to Us

　　很多很多人非常不恭敬地神（土地神之簡稱），甚至是自稱學佛的人，也有很多很多不恭敬，亦不「認可」地神的存在，以及有必要召請祂、供養祂。倘若妳、你是一般的人，沒人教妳、你，那是無可厚非的。對於那些有信仰，也已修行的人，還有這樣的態度，那就是一種無知，再加可憐。

　　佛教的教義，是最圓融無礙的。什麼叫最圓融無礙呢？是一切均包含。既是如此，佛教徒應不可，亦不會不認可、不恭敬、不供養祂們。再說，佛陀所證得的智慧，是平等性智，眾生皆有佛性。應無分別心才是，這樣也才是真正契合如來之聖教。

　　佛經裡皆可看到「安土地真言」，而我們在開始誦唸佛經前，也應唸「清淨咒」，然後就唸「安土地真言」。為何要唸這真言呢？因為地神顧名思義，就是最靠近我們的神靈。最靠近妳、你不請，難道妳、你要請幾個「星球」以外的「高靈」嗎？遠水如何能救得了近火？

　　玟瑚師父告訴妳、你，地神是真的很接近人類的，過去吾常幫客人做「謝土」儀式，就有一些客人不相信，或不大相信有地神這回事，地神知曉他們的「疑慮」，馬上就顯化一點「風吹草動」，向他們「打招呼」，實在是「靈」驗。

地神每戶家宅皆有，無論妳、你是什麼族群，祂就在妳、你家，相等於家庭成員，一切瑣事祂都能幫妳、你，請別忽略祂。

―――― 英譯 ――――

Many people show great disrespect towards the Earth Deity. Even self-proclaimed Buddhists disrespect and do not acknowledge the presence of the Earth Deity and the need to make offerings to Him. If you are like the common folks who are ignorant about this fact with no one to teach you, you might be excused. However if you have a religious belief and are already cultivating spiritually, yet hold this false tenet about the Earth Deity, you are indeed ignorant and pitiful.

The teachings of Buddhism are perfect and free of all obscurations. What does that mean? That the Buddhadharma is all-encompassing and includes all. Since that is the case, a Buddhist cannot and must not reject, show disrespect and refuse to make offerings to the Earth Deity. Moreover, the Wisdom of Equality that the Buddha has attained states that all sentient beings are equal and possess the Buddha-nature. Therefore we should not be discriminatory. In this way, we will be truly aligned with the essence of Buddha's sacred teachings.

You can find the mantra of Earth Deity in many Buddhist scriptures. Furthermore, before we start a mantra or sutra recital session, we should chant the purification mantra, followed by the mantra of the Earth Deity. Why is that so? The reason is because the Earth Deity is the nearest of all Deities to us. You cannot be ignoring the one nearest to you and go searching for a higher-level deity a few planets away! As the saying goes, "Water from afar is unable to douse the fire near at hand."

Let Master Dai Hu tell you this: the Earth Deity is really the nearest deity to us humans. In the past when I performed the Earth God Thanking rituals for my clients, some of them did not fully believe in the existence of Earth Deity. The Earth Deity at their house knew of their suspicion and would immediately manifest some external phenomenon to say "hello". How uncanny!

There is an Earth Deity in every household, regardless of race. He lives in your home, just like a family member. He has the ability to help you in all matters, big or small. Please do not ignore him.

登山觀浮雲
Watching the Clouds From the Mountains

　　記得年少時，很喜歡騎著吾那視如寶貝的越野車，往那不知名，渺無人煙的地方駛去。有時是和鄰居朋友，有時則是自己一個人。但吾比較喜歡獨自一個人。選擇一個人是因為，想要慢慢地，靜靜地，尋覓著過去人們留下的痕跡，以及大自然的美麗、寧靜、守時、誠信、貢獻，甚至是愛。描述大自然的這一段，並非年少時的感悟，而是長大學佛才有的「妙觀察智」。

　　吾的皈依師父說：爬山能鍛鍊體魄，也能培養一個人的耐力、毅力以及光明的身心。師父所說的，甚有道理。吾在十多年前，很喜歡和一位師兄到位於西南部的一座名山，欣賞大自然的鳥語花香，兼分享我們皈依師父的著作。如今已過了十多個寒暑，時間真的過得很快啊！還好吾並無浪費這十多年的光陰。玄學與佛法兩大超然智慧，同時積極研習，弘法利生，發揚玄學，清涼渡有情。

　　「登山觀浮雲」要表達的，絕對不是消極。而是一種融入大自然的智慧，一種積極將「小我」融入大自然之「大我」的真正智慧。若您不信「登山觀浮雲」有這般「神奇」，且讓吾向您娓娓道來吾「登山觀浮雲」後所得的智慧。

　　「登山觀浮雲」後讓吾領悟：

一、修行人必須時時觀照自心，勿使「心猿意馬」。

二、成、住、壞、空，真實不虛也。無論您在世間富或貧，勝或敗，美或醜，貴或賤，壽或夭，強或弱，喜或憂，一切都會過去的。

三、世間之一切，皆無常態。

四、修行要趁早，在一息不來前。

五、修行要依次第，欲速則不達。

六、修行要重德。天有德所以常覆，地有德所以常載。

七、打開心扉，讓陽光照進來。

您們看看，「登山觀浮雲」竟然能給予我們，如此之多的無價之寶。有了這些無價之寶，吾即「富有」，夫復何求呢？

做人本應該「簡簡單單」，生在這五濁惡世，已經夠苦了，又何必「急急忙忙」地將更多的「繩子」往自己身上套呢？當年禪宗二祖慧可大師，向達摩祖師求安心法門，達摩祖師反問慧可大師，祢把心掏出來，我幫祢安心。這時，慧可大師方才醒悟。自己的心要自己去安，而並非他人能安啊！世人都說苦，但世人從不安安靜靜的坐下來想，想一想苦從何而來，誰將苦給您，想到最後，您會發現，是自己「硬」把苦找來的，而並非誰給誰，誰綁誰啊！放下吧！人在世除了糊口以外，不妨學吾「登山觀浮雲」，參一參如何做一個真正快樂、自在、常樂我淨的人。感恩。

I remembered my younger days when I simply loved to ride my precious mountain bike to unknown remote places where there were little signs of habitation. Sometime I rode with my neighbours and friends, other times I went alone. I preferred to be on my own. My choice of solitude allowed me to slowly and peacefully explored traces left by past inhabitants. It also enabled me to discover the beauty of Nature, her peace, her punctuality, her integrity, her contribution and love. These descriptions of Mother Nature did not arise when I was younger. These came to being only after I learnt the Dharma and developed a contemplative wisdom of insight.

My Guru Master said that climbing the mountain will build one's physique, as well as cultivate one's patience, perseverance and a body and mind of illuminated clarity. What my Guru Master said makes a lot of sense indeed. More than ten years ago, I used to enjoy going to a well-known hill on the southwestern part of the island with a Dharma brother, to admire the rural idyll of Nature, as well as to share the Dharma books written by our Guru Master. More than ten seasons of Winter and Summer had passed. How time flies! It is a relief that I did not waste the past decade. The fields of Chinese Metaphysics and the Dharma are filled with superior wisdom. I research both studies diligently, propagate the Dharma to benefit the sentient beings, promote the wisdom of Chinese Metaphysics, and deliver sentient beings when the affinity arises.

The message that this article hopes to convey is definitely not of pessimism. It is about being in oneness with the wisdom of Nature. It tells of the pure perseverance of integrating our own consciousness and wisdom with that of the Universe. If you do not believe in the incredibility of Nature, please indulge me as I share with you the wisdom I gained from Nature.

The wisdom I gained from Nature:

1. A spiritual practitioner needs to be constantly aware and watch over his mind, and not let it wander and be restless.

2. The cycle of life and destruction (formation, existence, destruction, emptiness) is indeed true. In this worldly existence, you may experience wealth or poverty, success or failure, beauty or ugliness, nobility or lowness , longevity or short life span, happiness or sorrow, yet all these will pass.

3. The world is in a constant flux of change.

4. Spiritual cultivation must begin early as your next breath may not come.

5. Spiritual cultivation must adhere to a sequence. More haste, less speed.

6. The foundation of spiritual cultivation is dependent on the nobility of our character. Heaven and Earth is noble and all-encompassing.

7. Open up your heart and let the sun shine in.

Look at all the precious gifts endowed to us by Nature. With all these treasures in hand, I am already a rich man. What else more is there to ask for?

As human beings, we ought to live simply. Being born in this world, heavily tainted by the Five Turbidities, is more than enough suffering. Why is there a rush to entangle oneself with more ropes?

The Second Patriarch of the Zen Tradition, Reverend Hui Ke, seeked out Bodhidharma to ask for a way to ease his heart. Bodhidharma asked Reverend Hui Ke to hand over his heart so that He could ease it. At that moment, it dawned on Reverend Hui Ke that He was the only one who could ease His own heart, and not by others. The common people often complain of sufferings, but very few actually take some quiet time out to ponder deeply and search for the origin of sufferings. Who give you these sufferings? You will discover, after your deep ponder, that you are the culprit who force the sufferings upon yourself. Let it go! Besides working for your basic sustenance, you should get in touch with Nature, just like me, and contemplate on the way to become a truly happy, free, joyful and pure person.

My Gratitude to All.

給國家領袖的祝福
My Wishes for Our Country's Leader

　　大概三年前，吾算出這幾年內李光耀先生的健康將會亮起紅燈，所以告訴弟子要多留意他的消息，有什麼消息，要第一時間告訴吾。

　　上星期得知李顯龍總理要接受前列腺切除手術時，吾翻開農民曆查看他動手術的日子，看了之後，會心一笑。那日子對他有利，手術一定會成功。國家領袖背後應該也有高人指點。感恩。

　　在李總理的臉書賬戶上，有人祝福有人詛咒。而近日咱們的國父李光耀先生因感染嚴重肺炎入院，也一樣有人祝福有人詛咒。

　　當一個國家的元首或者領袖真的是非常非常地不容易，尤其是在我們新加坡。新加坡本身什麼天然資源都沒有，一切都要靠人力物力。國家搞得不好，財團哪會願意來這裡設廠，製造更多的就業機會呢？顧一個家庭就已經很難了，而領導者顧的是這麼多的人和事。吾看李總理上任不久後，頭髮都變白了，可見要耗的精神和承受壓力有多大。

　　身為一個「人」，應該是祝福一個「人」。如果你覺得他做得不好，你又何必象他一樣不好呢？開口詛咒人，你認為你就是好嗎？千萬不要，這樣顯得我們小氣巴拉，顯得我們沒有素養、沒有學養、沒有修養、沒有涵養。我們要做一

個有學養的人，要先去了解清楚。如果是你當家，你患上這種病例，那人家在詛咒你，「另類」地祝福你，你的感受會如何？大家要將心比心，這樣才是正人君子，這樣才是一個「人」。

世界各地沒有一個政府是完美的，只因這是人間。能夠生長在新加坡，已是一個大福報。很多國家都沒有比新加坡來得穩定繁榮。不要還沒有報國恩，就變成一個「負心」的人。在因果上，當你辱罵一個人的時候，其實你是在將你的福份大量地扣給那個人。

吾玳瑚師父祝福我們國家的李顯龍總理速速地康復，繼續地為國家謀取更好的福利，更希望國父李光耀先生能早日從病苦中解脫。

242

────── 英譯 ──────

About three years ago, I deduced that the health condition of Mr Lee Kuan Yew would show signs of deterioration in the coming years. I told my disciples to look out for any related news and keep me informed.

I got to know last week that our Prime Minister, Mr Lee Hsien Loong, was scheduled to undergo a surgery to remove his prostate gland. I checked the surgery date in the Farmers Calendar and was relieved that the date was beneficial to PM Lee. I knew that the operation was going

to be a success. He must have gotten sound advice on the date from advisers of high caliber. Thank goodness for that.

On the Facebook page of PM Lee, many left well wishes and there were some who made unkind comments. And recent news on our Founding Father, Mr Lee Kuan Yew, who got hospitalized due to pneumonia, attracted similar well wishes as well as unkind remarks.

It is a very arduous job to be the leader of a country, especially in Singapore. We do not have any natural resources and have to rely on human resources. If the country is not managed well, which consortium would want to invest in our country and where will our employment opportunities come from? To manage a family is challenging enough, let alone to run a country with a myriad of complex issues and people. I saw that Mr Lee Hsien Loong has turned silver-haired not long after he became the Prime Minister. One can imagine the amount of stress and mental exhuastion he had to undergo.

As a human being, we should have well wishes for another human. If you feel that he did a bad job, why follow suit? To curse someone does not make you any better. Please do not do that. It would make you seem like a petty person with no proper upbringing, values, self-control and education. We should be learned and understand the situation first.

If you are in his shoes, and you contracted similar illness, how would you feel to be on the receiving end of unkind comments? Please think about it like how a real gentleman would. That is how a human being should behave.

There is no perfect government in the world as this is the mortal world. To be living in Singapore is already considered a great blessing. There are many countries who do not possess our level of stability and prosperity. Do not be the heartless one who has not repay the privileges given by your country. In the eyes of karma, when you scold and humiliate a person, you are, in fact, transferring a huge amount of your merits to that person.

Master Dai Hu wishes PM Lee a speedy recovery, and may he continues to strive to better our country. It is also my sincere hope that Mr Lee Kuan Yew be free from the sufferings of ill health soon.

愚孝愚愛
The Ignorance of Fillial Piety and Love

　　大多為人父母的客人找吾，為自己或他們的子女批大運或流年時，均向吾「開門見山」地要求希望吾能大力幫助，圓滿他們對於子女的期望與厚望。天下父母望子成龍，望女成鳳，是無可厚非的。但成了龍成了鳳後，他們卻傲氣逼人、目中無人，自私自利、有進無出、對國家對社會毫無貢獻、將年邁父母送進養老院，祇是為了要和妻子或老公，過二人世界，等等。這樣的愛給予令千金令公子，是有欠妥當的。這種愛謂之愚愛啊！

　　成龍成鳳固然好，但若將之與忠、孝、義、悌、禮、儀、廉、恥，這八德來比較顯然尊卑立判啊！倘若妳、你告訴吾普天下這樣子的人難覓，吾就實實在在地回覆妳、你，就是萬中有一，才叫做尊貴啊！我們上一代所做的錯就不該也不願讓下一代繼續地錯下去，反而還得將正確的價值觀傳承於他們，使他們一生順遂與欣榮，這樣就是真愛、正愛。

　　很多為人子女者，認為賺多一點錢，帶父母去旅行，給父母住更大間的房子，帶父母上高級餐館用餐等等，就是孝順。吾則認為那是愚孝的範圍罷了。且讓吾分析給你們聽及看。每個國家都有其特定五行，倘若妳、你帶父母去的國家，五行為妳、你父母八字中的忌神，旅途中會發生意外、食物中毒、回來不只不能達到鬆懈身心的效果，反而生病破

財，請問這是否是明智之舉？

　　懷胎十月，生後還得照顧大小號、起居飲食等等。待他們老來時，我們依然在他們身旁，照料他們一切所需，並與之分享佛法，讓他們知曉百年歸去的去向，讓他們適時打造另一世界的家，才算是盡了孝道，天地共欽，愚孝改為正孝。

───── 英譯 ─────

Many clients, who are parents, engage my services to analyze the luck cycles of their children and themselves. They are frank about seeking my help to realize their high hopes in their children. It is natural that all parents in this world hope that their children have a bright future. But once the children achieve success in life, they become arrogant, disrespectful, self-centered, stingy and give no contribution to the society and the country. They would send their aged parents to the old folks' home, just so that they can enjoy a life with only their spouses etc. Such is the inappropriate love to shower upon your children, because it is just foolish love.

It might be very pleasing for the parents to see their child excelling in life. However, if you compare a child having external achievements with another child possessing the eight virtues of loyalty, filial piety, integrity, brotherhood,

manners, etiquette, righteousness and sense of shame, it is immediately obvious who stands out. If you tell me that such virtues are almost impossible to find in a person in this world, I will tell you frankly that precisely of its rarity that it deserves the utmost honor and respect! Just because the last generation has committed wrongs does not mean the next generation should and must repeat the same mistakes. Instead, we need to pass down the right moral values to our next generation, so that they will have a smooth and prosperous passage in life. This is the true and right love to give our children.

Many children feel that by earning more money and being able to afford more holidays, a bigger house, and more meals at expensive restaurants for their parents, etc, they are being filial. I personally feel that this is a very ignorant form of filial piety. Let me share my analysis with you. Every country in the world has their elemental inclination (the five elements of Metal, Wood, Water, Fire, Earth). Should you bring your parents to a particular country whose elemental sign clashes with that of your parents', misfortune is likely to happen during the trip, like accidents and food poisoning. Instead of having a nice holiday to relax your body and soul, you end up sick and losing money. Please tell me, is this a wise move after all?

After enduring a ten-month pregnancy and the pain of child

birth, our parents still have to take care of our meals, shelter, sanitary needs and well-being. When they become aged, we are still by their sides, taking care of their needs and sharing the Dharma with them. We want to prepare them with the knowledge of their destination after death, so that they have ample time to "build" their next home in another world. This is real filial piety, one that is honoured by the Heaven and the Earth, one that is noble and right rather than ignorant and blind.

感恩的真諦
The True Essence Of Gratitude

　　近期常有人對吾「開口閉口」道感恩，除了「受寵若驚」以外，直覺上對方似乎並不太理解，何謂感恩。

　　感恩不外是感謝對方施給我們的恩澤，再來就是以她他們爲榜樣，學習她他們正確的身、口、意，然後以此準則，傳承於下一代，這是眞眞實實的感恩。

　　感恩不是一個「口頭禪」，感恩不是這一分鍾後，下一分鍾就對妳、你的恩人「七情上臉」，或「還以顏色」。若是這樣的話，就不是感恩了，而是恩將仇報，也是忘恩負義的。這樣會敗德，我們的祖先也會遭殃啊！

249

　　感恩是從心底發出的，感恩不是口是心非的，感恩是要付出於行動的，感恩是一輩子的，感恩是永不變的，感恩是圖報的，感恩以外依然感恩，這樣才是感恩的眞諦。

──── 英譯 ────

Recently, I have been hearing many people saying that they are grateful to me. Beside being slightly taken aback by them, my instinct tells me that they do not quite understand the true meaning of gratitude.

Being grateful is not just about feeling thankful to the

person who have shown us kindness. We should also be following his or her example by learning from his or her right thought, action and speech and passing on these principles to our next generation. This is the true meaning of gratitude.

Gratitude is not merely paying lip service. Nor is it feeling grateful this minute and turning your back on your benefactor the next minute! If this is the case, there is no gratitude to speak of. You are, instead, repaying kindness with vengeance. This is the characteristic of an ingrate with wretched morals. Such non-virtuous behaviour will bring misfortune to our ancestors as well!

Gratitude should come from the bottom of our hearts, and not mere lip service. The gratitude must be translated into actions. It should always be remembered, for the entire lifetime, unchanged, undeterred and must be repaid. Such is the true essence of gratitude.

電梯受困記
Being Trapped in The Elevator

　　前天，前往一工業大夏勘察風水時，首次受困於其升降機中。

　　吾與學生們進入電梯時，忽心血來潮，問弟子：「這電梯安全嗎？」

　　弟子回應：「我每次搭這電梯，都ok啊！」

　　門一關，「普隆」的一聲，電源中斷，伸手不見五指。

　　剎那間，無助、無常的心緒悠然而生。

　　吾問學生們，如果今天就這樣遇難，一息不來，什麼錢財、什麼名利、什麼恩怨、什麼產業，還有什麼不能放下呢？你的家庭、你自豪的臉孔、秀髮、你的儲蓄，還會是你的嗎？

　　人間真的有什麼好爭呢？

　　人生無常，生命脆弱，修行要趁早。若不及時懺悔惡業，他日身陷地獄，眼不見天日，耳聞慘叫聲，身心受酷刑，永處如此黑暗中，為時已晚啊！

　　想想，這或許也是吾的因果報應吧！小時候，較頑皮，喜歡和一群朋友玩電梯，朋友會把電梯內的燈熄滅，我們就在黑暗中亂喊一番，無聊既無知。真是有因必有果，不可不相信此循環！

　　受困四十五分鐘，呼吸開始辛苦時，慶幸電工已抵達及

251

時拉開電梯門，解救我們三人。再一次看到陽光時，心中無比地感恩！人的心中如果一直都有大日的光明，黑暗永遠不會侵入，那是多麼地美好啊！

　　感謝客人劉先生及管理層的協助，更感謝那名解救我們的電工！

── 英譯 ──────────────

The day before, on my way for a Feng Shui audit at an industrial building, I got trapped for the first time in a freight elevator.

As I entered the elevator with my students, I had a sudden intuition and asked my disciple, "Is this lift safe?"

My disciple replied, "I take this lift every time and it works fine!"

The lift doors shut and with a sudden jerk, the power supply tripped and we were thrown into complete darkness.

Feelings of helplessness and impermanence arose in me.

I asked my students, "If we are to meet with a mishap and have to take our last breath today, what's there left of our so-called wealth, property, fame and personal grudges? Your

family, your looks and long hair that you are so proud of, your savings, will those still be yours?"

In this mortal world, what is there to fight about?

Faced with the impermanence and fragility of life, cultivation must begin early. If we do not repent for our past sins in time, should we land in the darkness of Hell, our eyes will never see the bright sunlight, our ears will only hear horrifying screams of terror and our bodies will undergo torturous punishment. It will be too late by then!

Looking back, this is probably my retribution too. I was quite mischievous as a kid. My friends and I would often play with the elevators. The taller one would turn off the fluorescent light tubes in the lift and amidst the darkness, a bunch of us would be screaming and shouting in mock terror. How juvenile and ignorant we were then! The law of cause and effect truly exist and we should not be denying it.

We were trapped in the elevator for a good forty-five minutes. Just as we felt slight difficulty in breathing, the technician arrived in time to pry open the lift doors, rescuing the three of us. It was with much gratitude as I stepped out into the warmth of sunlight. How good it will be if the brilliance of sunshine is omnipresent in the heart of every person and darkness shall never invade!

Thank you to my client, Mr Low and the building management for their assistance! And another big thank you to the electrician who rescued us!

蒼天是否變了心
Did the Heavens have a change of heart?

　　兒時的一次玩耍中，忽然驚覺自己的心跳加速，當時的吾腦海裡在想，這心跳是什麼一個東西，可否將它定住，不讓它跳動。於是吾就將氣提住，可是兩邊都不討好，且將自己弄得更不舒服。不過在那時候吾也發現到，原來心跳與呼吸，有著不可分的關係。與此同時，也頓感生命的脆弱。成長後，一步一步地用心鑽研，人類種種的符號及密碼，準備貢獻於一切眾生。

　　吾在成長的韶光中第一次聽到，上天有好生之德時，吾不是很明白，當然也談不上很懂得感恩上天。直到學佛，與實修佛法多年後，才懂得什麼叫做上天有好生之德，也才懂得如何感恩，上天好生之德之恩。總然這些年來，特別多的天災地難，吾不會手指著天，罵佛祖罵天公。因為，吾是一位學佛，且修行多年的修行人，早已對因果報應之事，有著深切的研究啊！吾的快樂、吾的自在、吾的攝召等等，都是佛所教啊！

　　若妳、你心中，有蒼天變了心這個疑問是平常無奇的。因為從來沒人教於你們，而你們也沒主動，沒積極地去研究，去探討。為了釋你們心中的疑，為了讓你們早日將心中的疑，轉成正知與正見，再從正知與正見中，修出更深厚的福德，吾現在就殷勤為你們解說。

向上善

255

當年佛教教主，南無本師釋迦牟尼佛，開悟成道後，隨即就想進入涅槃。天上最大的兩位天神，趕忙下降勸請佛陀，住世為吾等眾生，宣示成佛離苦得樂之真理。這兩位至高的大天神，就是我們所熟悉的大梵天王及天公玉皇大天尊是也。蒼天從來都沒變心，變心的是人類，殺、盜、淫、妄、酒全部幹盡，天災地難是人類，自私自利的行為所招來。吾百忙中辦茶會、法會及同修，就是為了延續你們的慧命，希望你們不會是災難中的一分子啊！

────── 英譯 ──────

During one particular playtime back in my childhood years, I suddenly found my heart beating very fast. I began to wonder what this phenomenon was and if I could stop the heart from beating. As such, I held my breathe in a bid to stop my heart but it turned awry and I felt worse than before. At that moment, I realized that my heartbeat and my breathing were inseparable. It was also then did I realize the fragility of life. As I grew up, I delved, step by step, into the various secret codes and symbols of humanity, ready to contribute to all sentient beings with this knowledge.

I first heard the phrase "Heaven is benevolent to all living beings" during those happy days of growing up. I did not fully comprehend it at that time and naturally did not feel much gratitude for the Heaven. Things changed when I

began learning and practicing the Dharma for many years. I finally understood that phrase and found gratitude for it in my heart. Even as many natural disasters struck us in the past few years, I did not point my fingers at the sky and start scolding the Buddha or the Heavenly Jade Emperor. As a spiritual practitioner of many years, of course I know and comprehend the Law of Karma. Buddha has taught and given me my happiness, bliss, and affinity with sentient beings!

If you harbour this doubt as to why the Heavens seem to have a change of heart, it is natural. This is because you have not been taught nor have you seek the right wisdom to dispel this doubt. To transform your doubts into the right knowledge and opinions and from there, allowing your wisdom and merits to grow through cultivation, let me give you an explanation.

The day Lord Sakyamuni Buddha attained complete enlightenment, He had wanted to enter into Nirvana immediately. Two great Gods from Heaven immediately descended to plea for Him to abide in the Saha world and expound, to all sentient beings, the great Truth to put an end to their sufferings. These two supreme Gods are Lord Brahm (Four-faced Buddha) and the Heavenly Jade Emperor, very well-known to many of us. The Heaven never has a change of heart. It is mankind who has. Man has committed acts of killing, theft, sexual misconduct, deceit and addiction to intoxicants. These acts and the selfish behaviour of mankind manifested into the natural disasters we are experiencing today.

I took time out of my busy schedule to hold events like the tea sessions and puja ceremonies, so as to grow your spiritual wisdom and in the hope that you will never be a victim in the next disaster that strikes!

銜接聖誕節的意義
Christmas Day-Connecting the Dots

　　先恭祝所有基督教徒及天主教徒的讀者們聖誕佳節平安快樂。

　　聖誕節，故名思義，是爲了紀念耶穌基督的誕辰。祂是爲了世人的福利而降生人間的聖人，可惜世人根本不能辨認祂是眞的。因爲福報不足，救世主在世間傳福音才短短三年，就遭世人如此殘酷的對待。但祂沒有責怪世人，還請求祂的父王寬恕他們的無明，並願意以自己的鮮血洗滌眾生的業障。耶穌基督的愛沒有分別心，還有很強的忍辱性。這是完全符合佛法所提倡的忍辱及布施波羅密。祂是眞的得道者。

　　宗教從天上界傳下來人間，在天界，是沒有不和的，是人才不和，不但吵吵鬧鬧，還干戈四起。所有宗教的神明，吾一概尊敬。到客人家看風水時，無論她他們供奉的是聖母瑪麗亞、耶穌基督、聖約瑟、紅財神等，吾都畢恭畢敬地向祂們合掌頂禮，只因平等，平等。

　　聖誕節並非是搞一些派對、聚會或尋歡做樂的節日。所有的基督教徒和天主教徒，包括世人，應該先懺悔，然後向妳、你的教主發一個善心善念，去做至少一件利益世人的善行。把妳、你的小愛化爲大愛。在此時，也應懺悔過去對父母、長輩和師長的不恭敬和不孝順，這樣子才能眞正地平安

和快樂，及眞正慶祝聖誕節。

First and foremost, I would like to wish my readers who are Christians or Catholics a Blessed Christmas.

Christmas Day, as the name implies, commemorates the birth of Lord Jesus Christ. He is a Saint who descended into this world to bring salvation to mankind, but alas, the people in his time were ignorant and unable to see His true self. There were insufficient merits generated for the propagation of the Gospel, and in a short span of three years, the Saviour was cruelly persecuted by the very flock He wanted to save. Lord Jesus, however, did not blame the people and even mitigated on their behalf to His Father to forgive their ignorance. He was willing to use His own blood to atone for the sins of the people. Not only did Lord Jesus displayed equality in His love, He also has a very strong threshold of endurance in the face of humiliation, which are totally aligned with the qualities of Endurance and Giving, two of the Six Paramitas in Buddhism.

Saints and deities descended from the Heavens to spread the Teachings, through different religions. In the Heavenly realm, they are the same teachings, with no conflicts or

disparity. These differences only exist in the human minds. Men have squabbled and even fought wars against each other in the name of religion. Even though I am a Buddhist, I hold deep reverence to the saints and deities of other religions. Whenever I am at a client's residence for Feng Shui audit, I would respectfully put my palms together and pay homage to the Saints (Mother Mary, Lord Jesus, Saint Joseph, Lord Ganesha etc.) at their altars. All in the name of Equality.

Christmas Day should not be a day of parties, gatherings and merry-making. Instead, this should be the day for all believers (Christians and Catholics), and non-believers alike (that includes everyone of us) to first repent our sins, and make a vow to the Saint or Deity, whom you worship, to do at least one good deed that will benefit this world. Expand the reach of your love beyond yourself and your close ones. At the same time, we should repent sincerely for our disobedience and insolence towards our parents, elders and teachers. In this way, we will be able to achieve peace and happiness. And only in this way, we will truly be celebrating Christmas Day.

慶生的意義
The Significance Of a Birthday Celebration

上星期日，農曆五月十八日，是吾根本上師蓮生活佛的佛誕。

吾到高島屋的日本蛋糕店買了生日蛋糕，特別挑選了一個美味可口的巧克力蛋糕。上面有各色的水果點綴，呈現在人的眼簾裡，是個豐富和希望的畫面。

當晚用餐後，吾也免費為餐館內的侍應生們提供問事，與人為善。有些問的人態度不好、誠意不足、禮貌不佳、同一樣的問題問了又問、始終半信半疑，有時問的人會給個紅包以表感恩，有時只有一聲謝謝，但既然鄒前來問，就是一個緣。只要有那麼一絲的機會傳達善的訊息，吾不願、不肯也不會放棄，更藉此教導身邊迷失的青年。說了，聽不聽就是他自家的事了。

之後，再用數小時訓練學生如何介紹自己的根本上師和解說佛法。

很多人慶生無非就是吃喝玩樂，但吾個人堅持在生日那天要做至少一件有意義的事，更何況是根本上師的佛辰。吾自認自己無能，沒有多少資糧供養祂，而根本上師的期望是吾能學以致用、利樂有情，所以吾努力地以這一生的行舉功德不斷來供養祂，感恩祂的教誨。

我們的生日是媽媽的痛苦日，辛苦懷胎九個月，才在那

一天把我們生出來。如果在生日那一天，只懂得慶祝自己的存在，而沒有做些增厚自己人生價值的事情，慶祝的意義何在呢？

Last Sunday, the 18th Day of the 5th Lunar Month, was the birthday of my Guru Master, Grand Master Living Buddha Lian Sheng.

I bought a birthday cake from a Japanese bakery at Takashimaya. I selected a delicious chocolate cake with a colourful assortment of fruits toppings, which convey a sense of hope and abundance to anyone who see it.

After dinner that night, I gave free consultation to the servers in the restaurant hoping to form more positive affinities. Some servers displayed poor attitude, a lack of sincerity and mannerism and kept repeating the same questions with suspicion to my given answers. Some gave me a red packet as a token of gratitude, while others left with a word of thanks. The fact that they came forward to me meant an affinity between us. As long as there is a small chance for me to propagate kindness, I do not want to miss it. I take this also as a chance to guide the lost young people around me. If they ignore my advice, it would be their own doing.

After that, I spent the next few hours teaching my students how to introduce their Grand Master and present the Dharma to others.

Typically, many people celebrate their birthdays with feasting and merry making. For my birthday, I would always intend myself to do at least one meaningful thing. Furthermore, that day carried much more significance as it was the birthday of my Guru Master! Admittedly, I do not possess much material wealth to make an offering to my Guru Master but I knew His greatest hope is for me to apply what I have learnt from Him to benefit other sentient beings. So I make a conscious effort to be very diligent in my work and with the merits generated from my endeavors, I offer to my Guru Master as my greatest present to thank Him for His relentless teachings.

The day we were born was the day our mothers underwent excruciating pain to deliver us into this world, after bearing us for nine tough months. If the only thing we do on our birthday is self indulgence and ignore the chance to do something meaningful and add real value to our lives, what significance is there in such a celebration?

緣
Affinity

　　很坦白的說，吾活到這把歲數，才開始認清「緣」這個字。這個「緣」字若妳、你真真正正，實實在在地認清它，你應該會有這幾個覺受。一，大日照破黑暗。二，妄念斷除。三，煩惱解脫。四，周身通暢。五，智慧大開，等等。這些覺受絕對不是逼出來的，而是妳、你經歷過漫長的人與事，一天一天、一次一次的分析之，最後自自然然所得的。

　　一個「緣」字，真的很了得。它能夠開啓我們對於人生，種種之謎題如，有與無、是與非、對與錯、苦與樂、悲與喜、健與病、富與貧，等等的智慧。有了這樣的智慧，我們才能得以高枕無憂、夜夢安甜（甚至無夢）、隔天晨起，心曠神怡、全身「電力」充沛。正所謂，「夜來風雨聲，花落不知曉」。哈！哈！哈！

　　最直接了當地說，吾從「緣」字裡所得的智慧，是珍惜與放下。或許妳、你會認為，又珍惜又放下，好像莫名奇妙。且讓吾為你們釋疑。善緣、逆緣，來者去者，皆欣然接受，謂之珍惜。一般人祇接受善緣，而拒絕逆緣，那是因為他們不諳因果，未得其中的智慧，見色起相。要知道，今世所受，乃累世所結也，諸位大德應做如是觀。當妳、你明了累世所結，妳、你就應該去「化緣」，化掉所有的恩怨情仇，使不平不滿的念頭得以圓滿平息，謂之放下。

265

吾，玳瑚師父，奉勸與勉勵諸位大德，好好地參這個「緣」字，早日掃除心中的垃圾，還妳、你本來清淨的「心靈」，永恆的快樂與自在，這才是不擇不扣的智慧。

───── 英譯 ─────

Frankly speaking, having lived till my current age, I finally got a clearer understanding of the meaning of affinity. Should you understand it in all its truthfulness and reality, you would have feelings and awareness akin to:

1. Darkness dispelled by the Great Light.
2. Total eradication of unwholesome thoughts.
3. Total eradication of all vexation.
4. Total relaxation of the body.
5. Growth in wisdom, etc.

These are not forced but are naturally brewed by your life experiences in people and things, day after day, retrospection after retrospection.

This word "affinity" is really something. It has the ability to inspire our wisdom to unravel the many puzzles of life: Have vs Have-not, Truth vs Untruth, Sufferings vs Bliss, Sadness vs Joy, Health vs Sickness, Wealth vs Poverty, etc. Equipped with this wisdom, we finally can sleep at ease

with sweet dreams (or no dream at all) every night, waking up the next day full of life and energy! As the saying goes, "Despite the thunderous night, one sleeps soundly through even as the flowers wilted under the rain".

Let's get straight to the point. The deep appreciation of affinity gave me the wisdom to handle all things in life: To cherish and to let go. Perhaps you may think that the above sentence is somewhat contradictory and strange. Let me explain. Affinities, be it positive or negative ones, come and go and we should accept and treasure them. Most people only accept the good affinities and reject the bad ones because they do not know the Law of Cause and Effect (Karma) and the hidden wisdom in it, thus forming their own false views based on what they see on the surface. Your sufferings in this life are attributed to your own doings in your past lives. Please apply this concept in your life, my dear readers. Once you understood the affinities that you have created in your past lives, you ought to go 'cleanse' each of them, to rid the ones of vengeance and hate, and lay to rest all unwholesome thoughts and grievances and finally let them go.

I, Master Dai Hu, advise and encourage my dear readers to ponder deeply on the word "affinity", and clear the trash in your heart to restore your soul to its original pure and pristine state, the state of eternal bliss and ease. This is, undoubtedly, true wisdom.

緣近緣遠，緣深緣淺
Affinity Near and Afar, Affinity Deep and Shallow

　　一個星期六的上午，吾和往常一樣，修了法準備「拳打腳踢」，手機鈴聲響起來，來電者是位多年的客人，是為其第三位孩子之名（吾撰之），難於抉擇及孩子的未來，想親自聽取吾的意見。可能是吾平時都有「護理」吾的耳朵，一接聽這位大媽的來電，講沒幾句，吾就驚覺她在哽咽。但畢竟這位大媽是堅強的，由開始到結束，她始終沒「放聲大哭」，要不然吾別想「拳打腳踢」也別想習禪修氣了。

　　玳瑚師父在此要告訴這位大媽，以及諸位大德，人與人之間存在著很微妙的前世，甚至多世的因因果果，當中的恩怨情仇，實難以說明，唯有宿命通（玄學包含在內）的人，才能明白個中因果，凡夫俗子根本無法明白的。這也是為甚麼，吾這麼多年來，依然老老實實學佛及玄學，就是要為你們解開，你們心中的「枷鎖」，讓你們得以釋放「塵封已久」，清淨快樂的「心靈」。

　　相信很多很多人，都有碰過自己並不十分想要見到的人或事。可是諸位必須得知道，有因必有果，萬般由不得我們，這也是宇宙循環的真理，妳、你祇要明白這真理，碰到再難搞的人，妳、你就不會因為她、他，而失去妳、你原本的自在。比如說，當妳、你遇見一位難搞的上司，妳、你要趕快想，這一定是妳、你上輩子先刻薄她、他，現在「輪」

到她、他來刻薄妳、你，這也就是吾剛才所說的因跟果，有欠就需還，這樣才叫公平啊！告訴妳、你哦！妳、你若想與她、他拼的話，這因果就無法「解」。妳、你下一世還要再與她、他「相約」娑婆哦！早還早自在，不是更好嗎？

其實這一切皆是緣，有些不請自來，是緣近，有些朝思暮想，欲親近之卻不得要領，是緣遠，有些在一起數十年光景，是緣深，有些祇見過一兩面，就不再聚首，是緣淺，緣近緣遠，緣深緣淺，皆是緣，那既然是緣，就「好聚好散」吧！何必「痛苦糾纏」呢？

英譯

One Saturday afternoon, I was going through my usual routine, completed a cultivation session and was about to start my "kick-about" session when my mobile phone rang. A client of many years was on the other line. She called to seek my opinion on choosing the names I crafted for her third child as well as the child's future. Perhaps I took good care of my ears because as conversation progressed, I realised that she was slightly choking with emotions. This client of mine was a strong woman and did not burst into tears during our entire conversation. If she did, I would have to say goodbye to my "kick-about" session, meditation & breathing practice.

I would like to tell this client as well as everyone that between each of us, there exists an intricate karmic link to our past lives and many lifetimes ago. Through these connections, we are bound by gratitude, suffering, love and hatred. It is very difficult to discern and only people with the ability to read the past existences (metaphysics practitioners included) will be able to offer an explanation of the cause and effect of each relationship. Mundane beings will find it impossible to understand. That is why I have, all these years, pursued the knowledge of the Dharma and metaphysics conscientiously, so that I can help open the locks in your hearts and release the trapped souls which are pure and joyful.

I believe that many of us have encountered people or situations that we would rather not. But lest not forget that every cause would have an effect, and it is uncontrollable. This is the law of the Universe. Once you understood this universal truth, you would not lose your inner peace when you meet that person, no matter how loathsome he/she may be. For example, should you work with a difficult boss, you must quickly realise that you must have ill-treated him in your previous life, thus now is his turn to return the favour! This is the law of cause and effect I have been talking about. If you owe something, returning it is inevitable. This is fairness! Let me tell you, if you decide to fight him, this karmic entanglement would not be resolved and you are

bound to meet him again in your next lifetime in this Samsara world. Is it not better to clear this karmic debt in this lifetime?

Actually these are all affinities. Some come uninvited, a sign of close affinity. Some affinities are so far that they cannot bear fruits even as we pine day and night for them. Deep affinities are those that bind us together for many decades. Shallow ones entails a couple of brief encounters and never to meet again.

Near or afar, deep or shallow, they are all affinities. Since it is affinity, let us be amicable when we meet and part. Why should we continue these entanglements in agony?

學佛
Learning Buddhism

　　一直都有這榮譽，讓很多男女有情，來向吾學習佛法。與其說來向吾學習佛法，倒不如說大家共參佛法。因為佛法浩瀚，就算窮盡我們一生，恐怕也難以學盡。所以吾說，大家共參佛法。吾並非謙虛，這乃是吾誠懇的一席話。

　　我是拜佛的，我是學佛的。這兩句話常有所聞。可是，您們知道嗎？拜佛和學佛，是完全不一樣的哦！根據吾多年的「明查暗訪」，那些人所謂的拜佛，是偶爾到寺廟上香禮佛、隨意供養、向佛菩薩禱告、傾述心事、祈求佛菩薩加持，等。在家沒看佛書，沒看佛經，沒修法，沒持咒，沒唸佛號，沒坐禪通明，沒守基本五戒，如；不殺生、不邪淫、不妄語、不偷盜、不飲酒以及沒……更「不可思議」的是，連皈依是什麼都不懂。又或者，還沒皈依。

　　學佛的首先，必須得認禮明師。這裡所謂的明師，是指有真實的證量，是大善知識，已明心見性。如此的明師，才會有法賦予我們。然後就要皈依佛、法、僧三寶。這樣才算是正式入門，成為佛弟子，依次第學習佛法。而佛弟子每日應做的，就是至少每日一修，閱讀佛經，閱讀佛書，唸佛，持咒，守五戒，行善布施，習靜坐，等等。哇！有無搞錯，這麼多功課。絕對無搞錯。若不這樣，根本不能說在學佛。您頂多可向人說，您是在拜佛。

　　當我們向他人說，我們在學佛，學佛本來就是學佛種種的好，種種的善功德，克期取證，覺行圓滿，成就無上正等正覺。貪、嗔、痴、妒、慢、疑，永斷，煩惱解脫，不受輪迴之苦，快樂，自在，任運，等等。這才是真正的學佛啊！佛法本就應該從生活中去實踐。離開生活，就沒佛法，離開佛法，就沒有生活。願大家仔細且再三思考。

　　當年偉大的佛陀，南無本師釋迦摩尼佛，為何要捨棄一人之下，萬人之上的權威，以及多少人夢寐以求的榮華富貴，而離城訪道、雪山苦行達六年、受千般萬般的魔難、千錘百煉，直至菩提樹下得證悟？這一切一切都是為了我們啊！人身難得今已得，佛法難聞今已聞，此生不將今生渡，更將何時渡此生。

273

　　我們學佛就是為了要成佛。但我們必須理清拜佛和學佛之差異，才能做一位清清楚楚的佛弟子，這才叫學佛。感恩。

────── 英譯 ──────

It has always been my privilege and honour all these years to have imparted the knowledge of Dharma to many men and women. Rather to say that I have taught them, I would like to view it as everyone of us learning the Dharma together. The Dharma is vast and expansive, limitless in fact. Even if we are to use every single moment of our lives, it will be impossible to fully comprehend the Dharma. Thus,

I am not being modest at all, in fact I cannot be more earnest, when I said everyone, including myself, is learning the Dharma together.

I pray to the Buddha. I learn the Dharma. These two sentences are quite commonplace. But do you know there is a distinction between them? According to my years of "investigation", those who said that they prayed to the Buddha merely visited temples occasionally to offer incense and pay their respect to the Buddha, some made some donations and prayed to the Buddha to ask for blessings. They did not study the sutras or other Dharma literature. Neither did they do any cultivation, chanting of any sorts, meditative practice, nor did they abide by the five precepts:

1. To refrain from killing living beings.
2. To refrain from taking that which is not given (stealing).
3. To refrain from sexual misconduct.
4. To refrain from false speech.
5. To refrain from intoxicants which lead to loss of mind-fulness.

And the most unfathomable of all, they have no idea of, or have not even taken refuge in the Three Jewels!

First and foremost, to start our journey to learn the Dharma, we need to identify an accomplished Buddhist guru as our

teacher. This Guru is one who has attained Enlightenment and is an embodiment of the Dharma itself. Only from such a Guru can we obtain the right guidance. We should then seek refuge in the Guru and the three Jewels (Buddha, Dharma and Sangha) to formally become a disciple of the Buddha and learn the Dharma according to a prescribed sequence. As a Buddhist, it is our duty to perform the following: daily spiritual cultivation, read the Sutra and other Dharma literature, chant the Buddha's name and mantras, abide by the five basic precepts, do good deeds and give generously, meditative practice etc. What! Are you kidding me? That is a long list of homework to do for a Buddhist! No, I am definitely not kidding you. Without this list of homework, you practically cannot say that you are learning the Dharma. At most, you can only tell others that you are praying to the Buddha.

When we tell others that we are learning the Dharma, it means learning all the virtues and merits of the Buddha and apply it on ourselves in order to attain complete Enlightenment and supreme Wisdom. It also means to sever the defilements like greed, hatred, ignorance, jealousy, arrogance, doubts and free one's mind from all troubles and attain true bliss, never to suffer from samsara again. This is the essence of learning the Dharma. The Dharma ought to be actualized in our daily moments of living. Away from our daily lives, there will be no Dharma. Away from the

Dharma, there will be no living. I hope everyone ponders deeply upon this.

In His time, why did the Supreme One, Namo Shakyamuni Buddha, forsake his power and authority which was only second to his Father, the King? Why did He forsake the great weath and fortune that many could only dream of? Why did He leave his royal birthright to seek the Truth, going through hardships and asceticism for six years, and countless calamities from the Mara, before finally attaining Enlightenment under the Bodhi tree? He did it for us, all sentient beings! It is a rarity to have the precious human rebirth. Just as it is difficult to obtain birth as a human, it is also extremely difficult to be born at the time when the Dharma is still present. Since we have both the favourable conditions in this life, we should seek an escape from samsara altogether. If not now, WHEN?

We learn Buddhism so as to become a Buddha. However, we need to clearly distinguish the act of merely paying lip service and the way it should really be: actualizing the Dharma in our daily living moments. Only then can we, without any doubt, become a disciple of the Buddha and learn the Dharma.

My gratitude to everyone!

學佛的出發心
Motivation for Learning the Dharma

　　午飯後小憩，想著度生的種種，對於眾生不認真學佛、不認真修法、不警惕自己勿重犯一樣的錯誤、終日顛倒妄想，等等。實在不勝唏噓啊！

　　回想自己當年為何要學佛，以及現在為何還在學佛，心中真實感恩吾的皈依根本上師，蓮生活佛盧勝彥。因為祂慈悲無私的教授、慈悲偉大的大加持，讓吾能實修佛法，漸漸將自己累世的習氣淡化及轉化，並守著當初皈依的出發心，因此，至今吾仍然學佛，且更積極更努力地學佛。那吾到底是以什麼為當初學佛的出發心呢？吾當初學佛的出發心是：

　　第一，尋求安心的法門。

　　第二，尋求能達於真善的法門。

　　第三，尋求能使自己不再造業的法門。

　　以上三點，是吾當初學佛的最至要的三個理由。吾的皈依師父教導我們，當邪緣至的時候，要趕快憶起當初學佛的出發心，就能抵擋邪緣。

　　吾個人認為，學佛弟子為何會退道心，原因在於學佛弟子並沒有將佛法實踐在日常生活中，也沒有勤修戒、定、慧，佛法中的三無漏學。就因如此，無法得到佛法，自然就無法「分辨真幻」，以至最終退了道心，學佛不成，反成了幽冥界悲慘眾生，真是哀哉！

　　很多人總以為，學佛辛苦又無聊。其實那剛好相反。皈

依學佛所受的五戒，事實是世間一切眾生均得守的五戒，而並非祇是皈依弟子才應守的戒律。因為，守五戒才能再得人身啊！再者，學佛知因果，更懂得行善布施、戒殺放生、言談舉止更為謹慎、廣修福田，不要說來世，這一世的命運，當下就改善了，從苦轉為順、從貧轉為富、從弱轉為強、從敗轉為勝，等等等。所以吾才說，學佛根本不苦，而且很樂。學佛也不無聊，學佛不再度日如年、行屍走肉、了無生機了。

學佛一定要拜對師父，一定要親近善知識。千萬不可人云亦云，道聽途說，這樣不但沒有功德，反而會有過失及罪。若妳、你與吾有緣，可以一邊品茗，一邊共參佛道，哈！哈！哈！真是人生一大樂事啊！

—— 英譯 ——

Taking a small break after lunch one day, I pondered over the various difficulties faced when teaching the Dharma to sentient beings. They are not serious, and do not caution themselves against committing the same mistakes over and over again. Their lives are lived in a perpetual state of delusion.

As I recalled the reason why I decided to learn the Dharma, and reflected on my perseverance till today, I am full of gratitude for the master I seek refuge in, Grandmaster Living Buddha Lian-Sheng. Because of His compassionate

and selfless teachings and blessings, I was able to practice the Dharma and gradually rid myself of unwholesome traits accumulated over many past lives. I remained steadfast in my faith and continue to practice the Dharma even more diligently.

What has been my motivation at the beginning of my Dharma journey? Firstly, I seek a practice that can set my worries and troubles at ease. Secondly, to seek a practice that can show me the door to true Bodhi. Thirdly, to seek a practice that will enable me to stop committing acts of negative karma. The above three points were instrumental at the start of my journey. My Grandmaster, in whom I seek refuge, taught that whenever we are beset with obstacles brought about by bad affinities, we ought to quickly remind ourselves of our initial vows and motivations to repel the obstacles.

In my opinions, many Buddhists lost their beliefs along the way because they fail to apply the Dharma to their daily lives. Neither did they diligently practice the Three Endeavors of Moral Discipline, Meditation and Resulting Wisdom. As a result, they cannot realise the value of Dharma and hence, lack the wisdom to see through the illusions. They subsequently gave up on the Dharma and sadly, join the ranks of suffering sentient beings in the nether world.

Many people assumed that learning the Dharma is tedious and boring. Well, it is exactly the opposite. The five precepts we observe after taking refuge are in fact applicable to all sentient beings, not just Buddhists alone. Because by observing these precepts, we can be assured of rebirth in the human realm for our future lives. Furthermore, the Dharma teaches the Law of Karma (Cause and Effect), and rightly encourages us to perform deeds of giving, to refrain from killing, and to be mindful of our speech and action. By accumulating such vast merits, there is no need to wait for the next life. We can change our current destiny right away. From treacherous to smooth-sailing, from poverty to wealth, from weak to strong, from losing to winning, etc. This explains why I said that learning the Dharma is not at all tedious, but a joyous journey. Learning the Dharma is neither boring nor hopeless.

To learn the Dharma, it is important to seek the right Master and to be around wise people. Do not follow the crowd blindly or rely on hearsay as not only will this fail to accumulate merits, it will also deepen your negative karma. If you and I have the affinity, let's explore the Dharma over a tea session! Ha! Ha! Ha! What a great joy in life that will be!

樹兒的低語
The Gentle Whispers Of The Trees

　　有一條快速公路，任妳、你載吾千百回，吾都不會有任何異議。其實不要說千百回，就算是萬回，吾也不會覺得厭倦。嘮！到底是哪條快速公路，有這麼大的魅力，能贏得咱們玟瑚師父的「芳心」呢？是朝往新加坡樟宜國際機場的東海岸快速公路。

　　小時候的吾，很是怕黑，夜間洗澡，有時還得勞煩吾之五姊，在衛生間外相陪，真是膽小。甚至有時候大姊夫載吾之雙親，及幾位兄弟姊妹，到外頭用晚餐或宵夜，車子經過多樹的地段，吾也會「渾身不自在」。但現在妳、你若把吾，置放在沒有照明的空房裡、衛生間裡、樹林裡……，吾已能「掌控大局」，自在且陶醉在其中。能有這麼大的轉變，皆因佛的智慧，「妙觀察智」。

　　吾獨愛東海岸快速公路，是因為其兩邊的大樹。每當吾乘坐的車駛過，它們總是親切的向吾「揮手」，說著吾聽不懂的語言。但因吾是玄學家，多多少少都懂得，去感應人、物及空間的磁波，因此吾曉得，它們是在與吾打招呼，並非常歡迎吾的蒞臨。當然禮貌上，吾也一樣親切的，回它們一個微笑。

　　久而久之，它們的話閘子也就打開了。它們是一個很龐大的家族，它們很滿意它們的「住所」，祇是這些年，路上的車輛迅速增長，車輛所排出的廢氣，著實讓它們「吃不

281

消」。它們知道吾爲它們難過，反勸吾不必難過，且要珍重自己，因爲它們的飲食，比起我們人類，可謂天然多了。很感謝「樹兒的低語」，且讓吾再向它們學習，更堅強、更無私的奉獻。

英譯

There is a particular expressway that, no matter how many hundreds of times that you ferried me through, I would have no slightest of objection. Even if it were a thousand times, I would not feel a single sense of tiredness. Wow! Which expressway holds such enchantment over me? Well, it is the East Coast Parkway Expressway, or ECP in short.

When I was a little boy, I was very afraid of the dark. During my nighttime baths, I would, at times, trouble my 5th sister to stand guard outside the bathroom. How timid I was. Even at times when my brother-in-law ferried my parents and my few brothers, sisters and I for dinner outside, I would cower in uneasiness as the car passed by areas with lots of trees. However, now, if you put me in an unlit room, toilet or forest... I am now able to be in control, and would indulge in the moment blissfully. I attribute such a massive transformation in me to the Buddha Dharma, the Wisdom of Observation.

I am particularly enchanted by the ECP because of the two rows of luscious trees lining the entire stretch of the road. Every time the car I am in drove past, they would "wave" at me in a heartwarming manner and speak in a language unknown to me. As I am a Metaphysicist, I can invariably sense and interpret the energy fields of the people, space and energy around me. Thus I know that the trees are acknowledging and welcoming my presence. I would also give them a smile as a form of courtesy.

After sometime, they began to communicate more with me. They are a mammoth family and are very happy with their place of "residence". It is just that the last few years had seen a rapid increase in the number of cars traversing the ECP, and they seemed to be struggling with the increased amount of exhaust fumes. They know that I feel sad for them, but in return, they advise me not to feel that way and to take care of myself instead. Their food source, compared to us humans, is much more natural. I am very grateful to the gentle whispers of the trees, which have taught me much of their ways of perseverance, humility and unselfish contribution.

國家圖書館出版品預行編目資料

向善向上／玳瑚師父著.－－二版.－臺中市：白象
文化，2017.03
　　面：　公分
　ISBN 978-986-358-470-4（平裝）

224.517　　　　　　　　　　106001606

向善向上（二版）

作　　　者　玳瑚師父
校　　　對　季謙
發 行 人　張輝潭
出版發行　白象文化事業有限公司
　　　　　　412台中市大里區科技路1號8樓之2（台中軟體園區）
　　　　　　出版專線：（04）2496-5995　　傳真：（04）2496-9901
　　　　　　401台中市東區和平街228巷44號（經銷部）
　　　　　　購書專線：（04）2220-8589　　傳真：（04）2220-8505
出版編印　林榮威、陳逸儒、黃麗穎、水邊、陳婉婷、李婕
設計創意　張禮南、何佳諠
經紀企劃　張輝潭、徐錦淳、廖書湘
經銷推廣　李莉吟、莊博亞、劉育姍、李佩諭
行銷宣傳　黃姿虹、沈若瑜
營運管理　林金郎、曾千熏
印　　　刷　基盛印刷工場
初版一刷　2015 年 10 月
二版一刷　2017 年 03 月
三版一刷　2022 年 02 月
定　　　價　280 元

白象文化　印書小舖 PressStore 出版難親　出版‧經銷‧宣傳‧設計
www·ElephantWhite·com·tw　f 自費出版的領導者　購書 白象文化生活館